KNOWLEDGE IS OF NO VALUE
UNLESS YOU PUT IT INTO PRACTICE

ANTON CHEKHOV

MEDITATIONS
——— of a ———
MODERN WARRIOR

TO
MARK

100%

STAY DANGEROUS

Rock

MEDITATIONS
—— *of a* ——
MODERN WARRIOR

Paul 'Rock' Higgins CAS, SAC DIP

AuthorHouse™
1663 Liberty Drive
Bloomington, IN 47403
www.authorhouse.com
Phone: 1-800-839-8640

© 2012 by Paul 'Rock' Higgins CAS, SAC DIP. All rights reserved.

No part of this book may be reproduced, stored in a retrieval system, or transmitted by any means without the written permission of the author.

Published by AuthorHouse   11/08/2012

ISBN: 978-1-4772-4167-7 (sc)
ISBN: 978-1-4772-4168-4 (e)

Any people depicted in stock imagery provided by Thinkstock are models, and such images are being used for illustrative purposes only.
Certain stock imagery © Thinkstock.

This book is printed on acid-free paper.

Because of the dynamic nature of the Internet, any web addresses or links contained in this book may have changed since publication and may no longer be valid. The views expressed in this work are solely those of the author and do not necessarily reflect the views of the publisher, and the publisher hereby disclaims any responsibility for them.

Contents

How We Look 1
Close Quarter Combat for the Close Protection Officer 3
Reflect 8
Awareness 9
Personal Security 12
Close Protection Combat Systems the Lowest Threat Level 15
Plan Your Training 20
Third Party Defence 23
Low Light Training 27
Warriorship 32
Behind the Times 35
Physiology 38
Speed 42
Speed 2 45
The Perfection of Technique Through the Totality of Presence 49
Edged Weapons 52
Edged Weapons 2 57
Close Range Gun Attacks 61
Vehicle Security 68
Pre-Post Fight Mental Battle 71
Home Security 74
Combat Focused 80
Looking for Wolves 86
Actuality Training 91
Programming the Mind 93
Pausing for Effective Combat 96
Discipline and Motivation 99
Force on Force—Realistic Scenario Training 102
Compartmentalization and the Art of Disambiguation
    (Split Personality) 105
Kidnapping and Hostage Taking 109

Improvised Explosive Devices 112
'The Now' 121
'On Winning' 123
'Bug—Out Bags' 126
Arcs of Observation for Executive Protection 130
Survival Training 136
Ranges 139

How We Look

How we look says everything about you as an individual, either as a civilian going about your daily business or at work and especially as a police officer, soldier or bodyguard for example. It also says something about if you work in a team, again as a police officer, soldier, bodyguard, security officer etc.

Apart from the opportunist who attacks on instinct on the spur of the moment, predators will often survey their intended targets. This not only happens in the civilian world, but also in the police, military and security world.

Your drills and focus need to be the same at your leisure time as they are at your work. This is not paranoia, just common sense.

We shall start off this discussion by looking at "dress". Whatever your dress code is, it can either help or hinder you in a "contact" situation if it has not been thought about and worn correctly.

Do you train in the same type of clothing you wear everyday or the same as you wear at work?

Is your base style a kicking style or a grappling style, if so does how does your base style perform in your choice of dress? If your base style employs lots of high kicks and you wear trousers or jeans that don't allow this, do you have a backup system that compensates for this?

If you are a grappler are your shirts and jackets loose enough to allow you to move freely.

If you struggle to move in your everyday or work cloths, then in a "contact" situation your performance will be seriously impaired.

How about all you ladies who train. Do you train in short skirts and high heels, or long skirts and dresses? Not only practicing defensive techniques but training to be able to take off your shoes and running while having to defend yourself.

If you are a police officer, soldier or bodyguard do you wear your belt order, fighting order or any other equipment with CQC in mind?

Bulky equipment like belt or fighting order, chest rigs, tactical vests and body armour can impair movements, so your training and combat strategy must reflect what you wear.

Like I said at the beginning, how you look speaks volumes about your professionalism either at work or leisure by sending the right signals to any bad guys who may be targeting you.

Training for real in realistic conditions in similar clothing that you will wear to work and in your leisure will highlight glaring floors in your defensive and offensive game plan, especially if you only train in gym kit.

I hope this gives you some points to think about in your training.

Next time we will take this a step further and look at how to sit and stand correctly if a potential attacker is in front of us.

Close Quarter Combat
for the Close Protection Officer

Taking "How we look" to the next stage we are going to progress to how we should sit and stand, but before we do I would like to digress a little, the point of this will become clear later. Everything we do in CQC follows a few simple formulas, one of them being:

We go from A to B by the most direct route.

We do not go from A to B via C

Let's take one analogy that everyone should be familiar with, the untrained fighters haymaker punch. This punch starts off at A and instead of going in a straight line to B, it goes in a curve through C, D and probably through a few more letters of the alphabet before it gets back to B.

OK Simple enough.

Throughout our life we perform the same everyday actions that every other person performs. These actions, whether it be sitting, standing or moving need to be practiced correctly until they become second nature.

We shall look at sitting first. Look at the photos of the two people sitting down, each position is totally different. When our reactions are measured in fractions of a second everything we do has to be correct. Let's break each position down and see how we establish the correct sitting position.

The person sitting on the left (position A) is sitting straight backed with his backside at the rear of the seat. The head is high and looking forward. The hands will either rest on the arm rests (if the chair has any), rest on the thighs or clasped together in the lap, as is the case here. The legs are shoulder width apart and the feet are flat to the floor. The body's weight is to the rear of the body making movement of any kind difficult.

Now let's break down position B on the right. He is sitting slightly forward, away from the rear of the seat. The head is in line with the spine but is more relaxed. The right leg is pulled back under the seat and the heel is raised off the floor. The left leg is forward of the body, bent at the knee and the foot is flat to the floor. The left forearm is placed on the left thigh and the right palm is placed on the right thigh just in front of the jacket. Weight from the upper body is evenly distributed between both arms. The body weight is central allowing movement in any direction. By using the above formula we can see which position is ideal for us.

Before you read any further try this experiment: adopt each position and simply stand up. You will see how quickly you can react from position B compared to position A.

Did anyone notice how Prince Charles bodyguard was sitting when Prince Charles he was attacked on stage in Australia?

Know we have looked at both sitting positions lets look at their tactical values.

Position A

Every movement from position A to standing up telegraphs our intent, this may only be fractions of a second but to a trained fighter who will see this, that's all they'll need. This is because essentially we are sitting in a squat position. Try standing straight up from this position without moving any appendages first, not very easy is it. The body is square on which gives a potential aggressor any number of the body's target areas. There is no lateral movement, you have to stand up first before moving off to one side, so intercepting anyone from an angle is seriously impaired. As you can see sitting like this has no tactical value.

Position B

In position B the upper body is covered by leaning forward and facing at a 45 degree angle. When standing up there are no prior movements so our intent is not telegraphed. Lateral movement is enhanced by the positioning of the feet. The front hand can be used to fend off as we stand up. If we are armed the drawing of a weapon is facilitated by the right hand resting at the top of the thigh near the jacket, this is the correct position for a hip or shoulder holster.

Let's do the same for standing as we have done for sitting. Look at the photo of the two people standing; again we have two very different positions. We will look at the one the left, position A first. This is the typical bouncer's stance. The stance is square on with the hands held either down by the sides, clasped in front of the groin or even clasped behind the body. The legs are shoulder width apart with the feet flat to the floor. The body's weight is evenly distributed onto both legs.

The person on the right, position B is standing at a 45 degree angle but the head is looking forward and the hands are held down by the sides. The right leg is to the rear with the body's weight on it. The left leg is forward of the body and both feet point at a 45 degree angle, the same as the body.

Let's look again at their tactical values.

Position A

All the body's target areas are facing any aggressor standing to the front. The feet being flat to the floor offer no movement in any direction without it being telegraphed. There is no balance in any direction. If we are armed the drawing of a weapon must include a full body movement to get into the right position, again telegraphing our intent.

Position B

All the body's target areas are facing away from any would be aggressor. The triangle that the feet form gives you balance and movement in any direction, whether voluntary or involuntary. The front arm is protecting the mid section of the body and can be brought up to fend off if needed. The rear hand is in the correct position for attacking, defending or drawing a side arm and the body is in the correct position for this drawing technique, hence no telegraphing of our intent. Position B does not give off an aggressive attitude, it looks none aggressive and calm while still being a ready stance.

The correct sitting and standing positions outlined above have been described for right handed people. Left handed people obviously adopt an opposite position.

The mind is like a computer, the more information we give it the longer it will take to come to a conclusion when asked a question. Our question regarding the above positions, is what is the best position and how does it give us the best tactical advantage. The more positions we have the longer our reactions will take. We can and should adopt position A as our preferred stance, those of you who work with firearms or have worked with them will have used position A when standing naturally with a weapon (long or short). Adopting this stance enhances our reaction time and is easily adapted to all situations. Try all the positions for yourself, have someone push you, pull you, rush at you and try to get past you. Feel how your body / balance reacts to each situation.

As we have to be realistic in CQC, you cannot expect to stand / sit in these positions indefinitely, as we are constantly moving, observing etc. we only need to adopt these specific positions when we perceive a threat or are uncomfortable with unknown persons near us. Until we become accustomed to adopting these positions subconsciously it is a good idea to stand and sit in these positions as much as possible.

There is of course is lot more to the above than we can cover hear, for instance we have hand positioning, movement, balance, environmental awareness to name just a few. Nothing can beat the physical practice of any form of CQC, but I hope that this has got you thinking about your own actions and drills while you are working and at your leisure.

Reflect

Does your training reflect the violence that occurs in your neighborhood?

Regardless of the style of close quarter combat that you train in, the majority of your training should be geared towards the current threat in your local area.

If there is a large amount of knife crime there is little point in doing lots of ground work or grappling.

If you live in an inner city high rise tenement block with narrow stair wells and lifts and has a high rate of robberies, or in an area with high car jacking crime then working on adverse situations should take up the majority of your training.

As a security professional I frequently travel the globe to various countries from moderately safe countries to those with high levels of violence and either hostile or potentially hostile environments. The close quarter combat training prior to deployment always reflects the levels and types of violence that is occurring in that location.

As crime threats in your area change then so should your training. For example you may have knife crime, then a spate of gun crime or a spate of kidnappings or robberies, as each trend comes and goes then your training should change to reflect these changes.

Awareness

Over the last year the levels of violence in the UK has risen largely due to the fact that sentencing of criminals has become non-existent, with crimes being given a lower rating to justify asbos, cautions and community service.

Seriel criminals are at large doing whatever they please with the knowledge that whatever they do the justice system will protect them more than their victim.

It has never been more important for the law abiding citizen to be able to protect themselves.

With violent crime being reported daily in the newspapers and on news channels it is still surprising how many people are unaware of their environments as they go about their daily business (see stats below).

This year there has been a large spate of murders and robberies which were committed near or outside of the victim's home, and with vehicle security technology making it harder for thieves to steal them, car jacking has seen an increase as thieves find it easier to employ violent attacks to acquire vehicle keys.

So why are people still walking around with their eyes wide shut?

For the most part statistically the chance of anything happening to you is quit slim. By this I mean being murdered or mugged, not your run of the mill Saturday night drunken violence. I really believe the "it won't happen to me" mentality is still prevalent in today's society.

Even if a large percentage of attacks are committed by the opportunist they must still spend a small amount of time planning the attack. Either choosing the victim, location, time and method of attack and obviously the awareness of the victim at this late stage of the attack is at zero. Not noticing someone walking in the same direction as you or towards you when the streets or paths are deserted, during the day or the night. Or worse noticing someone and not doing anything about it because "it won't happen to me". The alarm bells should have started ringing.

Our awareness procedures need to be utilized long before we get ourselves into the conflict stage of self protection, and this must start at home.

Whatever you are doing when you next leave the house, your safety will be enhanced by taking the time to do some research, unsafe areas, violent pubs and clubs, public transport times and routes etc. Obviously you would do more research if you were going to another town, city or country for example. As you can see some prior planning can cut down your chances of not becoming a victim.

But this is only the first stage. While out and about there are a huge amount of skills to be employed to keep yourself out of harms way. The short list below is only a handful of the skills you should be aware of to keep yourself from getting to the conflict stage.

Body language
Colour codes
Where to sit on public transport
Which side of the road to walk on at specific times of the day.
How do you park your vehicle
How do you approach your vehicle in multi story car parks
How do you approach corners

These are just a few of the basic skills we employ to keep us ahead of the game. We need to give ourselves a much time as we can to react, because reacting to our environment is what we have to do.

Look at this formula for self protection.

DETECT—EVADE—AVOID—DEFEND

First we detect the threat—research

We then evade the threat—see the threat before an attack takes us by surprise

Avoid the threat—talking, walking, running, driving ourselves out of the attack vicinity

Defend ourselves from an attack—when all our other procedures have failed

Going through the above gives us a good chance of not being taken by surprise, which is what an attacker is after in the FIGHT—FREEZE—FLIGHT part of conflict.

The stats from the Mail Online report that someone is attacked in the UK every 30 seconds, with 50% of attacks being carried out by strangers.

There were 1,057,000 violent attacks last year
2,895 per day
120 every hour

And these are only the reported ones.

For all the unaware out there I hope your physical skills are up to speed because with the stats listed above it is just a matter of time before "it won't happen to me" happens to you.

Personal Security

As I write this newsletter there is a foot of snow on the ground, freezing fog and the daytime temp is down to -7 the night time temp on average is between -10 and -15°.

Traveling in this and in worse conditions can turn into a nightmare for the unprepared.

At times like this how often do you think of your personal security?

Travel security is just one fact of your personal security plan and in extreme weather conditions, planning is essential when traveling by road.

I live in a rural location 20 miles form the nearest town, the last thing I need is to be stranded between both locations with very little mobile phone coverage. Either way it is a long walk, if the weather allows me to walk at all.

Having a check list is the easiest way to prepare yourself, and in time you can build up a collection of checklists to cover most contingencies.

Meditations of a Modern Warrior

This example of a winter checklist is for traveling short distances in these conditions.

<u>Personal</u>

Weather check completed
Warm clothes
Waterproof boots
Hat and gloves
Breakdown / rescue Telephone numbers

<u>Vehicle</u>

Fuel	OK
Oils / Coolant	OK
Screen wash	OK
Tyre tread	OK
Jack and tyre iron	OK
Spare wheel	OK
Lights	OK
Maps	OK
Grab Bag	Shovel
	Blankets
	Tow rope
	Matches
	Candles
	Torch

<u>Kit</u>

Charged mobile phone—in car charger
Thermos flask
Food

This short list for traveling locally would not be applicable if you were driving to the Alps for a winter holiday, you might consider among other things:

Sat nav—vehicle and personal
Snow chain—vehicle and personal
Emergency telephone numbers   Police
                                   Hospitals
                                   Ambulance—vehicle and air

Major first aid kit
Two way radios
Spare clothes

The list you make can be as in-depth as you like and will be specific to where you are going and what you are doing and will also depend on the time of year you are traveling.

A little planning could save your life. How many times have you see / heard of people dying, stranded in their vehicles in serious blizzard conditions. You might think "it won't happen to me" but for those of you who are familiar with Murphy's Law, it might just happen.

So do a little planning and have a safe, happy and prosperous New Year.

CLOSE PROTECTION COMBAT SYSTEMS THE LOWEST THREAT LEVEL

Before we can train to counter any threat we have to look at that threat and its variants closely so we can implement the right responses.

The lowest level of threat facing The CPO and the client comes from the nuisance person. This can be one of the most problematic threats to cope with out of all the threat levels we may face.

This is due to the fact that the person being a nuisance is offering us no visible signs of violence.

The responses to this threat and its variants are less defined than in an outright physical attack and pose us two problems.

The first is if we respond to aggressively we may cause embarrassment to our client, especially if there are reporters and cameras around.

The second problem is that if we do not respond firmly enough the nuisance person will carry on being a nuisance. This again can cause embarrassment to the client and in the clients eyes may look like we cannot do our job. Hence no more job.

This brings us to what we are really protecting at this threat level. That is the public image of the client. Protecting their image from the media, protecting their image from the public, and protecting their image from their friends.

In a physical encounter as long as your client is rendered safe and unharmed, or relatively unharmed any embarrassment that may have been caused will probably be overlooked.

The Standard Operating Procedure (SOP) for a team dealing with this threat is to give all round body cover and walk through/past the threat, with the nearest c/s dealing with the threat. That is straight forward enough; the difficulty is in how the c/s dealing with the threat deters them, that subject is for another time.

First we have to look at who we class as a nuisance and then how we should measure our responses.

We all know what a nuisance person is and I am sure we have all had to deal with them at some point in our private lives so I will leave out the dictionary explanation.

A physical attack will have to be repelled no matter who the client is. But what might be a nuisance to one person may not be to another. Only by working with the client will you be able to determine who and what constitutes a nuisance to them.

For the purpose of this article we will look at a general group of people who could be possible nuisances to clients.

These are reporters, photographers (paparazzi), fans, beggars and drunks. We will look at each one in turn but they all have certain things in common. What they want is the client's valuable time and to get this they will appear unannounced, can be rude, they may impede your movement, they will or they will try to invade yours and your client's personal space. They will do this by crowding you, trying to get between you and your client. They will be pushing cameras, microphones or tape recorders into your clients face, pens and paper for autographs or hands for money.

We have all seen the celebrity bodyguard and I use the term lightly here, pushing fans and photographers around and to the ground. This lack of training and standard of behavior does not do the reputation of the client any good at all. This response definitely is not in line with the threat posed.

This example can be used to formulate a series of responses. Various levels of response can be attached to each different nuisance person. As part of your job keeping files on all threats to the client is essential and will help in formulating response plans. Part of the response plan will also depend on the size of the team you are working with or if you are an Individual Bodyguard (IBG).

Response plans can only be formulated once you know what type of threat you are facing. So we will briefly look at each group individually.

Reporters

Depending on who the client is will usually dictate how a reporter will approach them. Do they respect the client, do they like him, is he well known to them, IE: has he had amicable or inflammatory dealings with them in the past. How does your client view the reporter's. What are the circumstances that the reporter is dealing with, does your client want to answer any questions at all.

In certain circumstances reporters can be as pushy as photographers as they want to get their all important questions answered.

Remember, reporters do not intend any physical harm to the client so your response must reflect this.

Photographers

As with reporters, photographers are not offering any physical harm to your client, they are after taking a photograph. However we personally feel about them our response must reflect this. Again depending on who the client is will dictate how the photographers respond to them. Is your client a volatile person, the more wound up your client gets the better for the photographer's. Are you looking after a female? The more intimate the photo the more money the photographer makes. Remembers what you are protecting, the clients image. Your responses may be different for both the above examples.

Fans

Fans can generally fall into two types. The emotionally uncontrolled screaming fan and the quiet well behaved type. Both need to be dealt with differently while still keeping them fans of your client. The first type of fan is usually more of a danger to themselves and those around them than to you and the client, though sudden headlong dashes towards the client are not unheard of.

Obviously the respectful fan is a lot easier to deal with and easier to control.

Two people will have the final say in who approaches the client. The Team Leader (TL) and the client themselves. Your client may like meeting fans of all types and handshakes, autographs and gift giving can cause problems you must be prepared for.

Beggars

Today in any large city and especially in London we get different types of beggar. These range from the homeless sitting with a cup in front of them not bothering anyone, to buskers and the ones we are interested in. These are the Eastern Europeans. These beggars are female and come with children in tow and in reality are not beggars in the true sense as they are controlled by Eastern European organized crime gangs who collect whatever money these women get from begging. The beggars will follow and pester you until you give them something unless they are dealt with quickly.

This type of beggar can quickly escalate from nuisance person to a physical attack. They have been known to spit on people who refuse to give them anything and when begging from females they have been known to punch and push them to the ground.

Drunks

All of the above groups of people tend to focus their attention on your client. These people are the ones who will also focus their attention on the bodyguards. They will see the bodyguard as the target not the client. They will see the bodyguard as the "hard man" they will want to test themselves against you and from starting with taunts can quickly escalate to aggressive physical attacks.

In their drunken state they think it will bring them great kudos to say to their friends "I dropped so and so's bodyguard". Because of their inebriated state it is very hard to reason with them and in any case you will probably not have the time to do so. As I mentioned at the start of this article the standard practice for this level of threat is all round body cover and walk through, this to them is seen as you running away and will often just end in more drunken abuse being hurled in your general direction.

So looking at the above variants to the threat of the nuisance person you may need to formulate response plans to correspond with each specific attack variant, and when you look at the other threats listed below you can see how different your response plans will be as you go from the lowest level of threat to the highest. But don't forget that each specific threat also has its large number of attack variants and your responses will also be different depending on whether you are armed or unarmed.

THREATS

Nuisance Person
Verbal Assault
Missile Thrown
Hostile/Friendly Crowd
Unarmed Physical Assault
Armed Physical Assault
Close Range Gun
Long Range Gun (Sniper)
Bomb or Grenade Attack
Vehicle Ambush

Plan Your Training

A report from 2006 stated that boots are more harmful than weapons in street violence. It stated that preventing attacks involving kicking and blunt objects is as important as preventing knife attacks, and how right it is.

With the increase in knife violence over the past couple of years, this report is still as valid now as it was then. Compare how many people you know who have been in an unarmed street fights to those who have been involved in violence where weapons have been involved. In most fights it is still the fist, head and boots that are the main weapons, although we always expect our adversaries to be armed.

The report states that the feet are more likely to cause severe injury than any other method of assault. The statistics were arrived at over a period of six years, by reviewing treatment of violent actions at the University Hospital Wales.

Although an assault with a weapon is generally more likely to cause severe injury than a none weapon assault, kicking was the single most likely method to cause severe injury.

Other most likely methods were, in order:

Blunt objects
Head
Sharp objects

Despite being the most common weapon used, fists are the least likely weapon to cause severe injury.

The report also found that there was little difference between injuries inflicted by one or two assailants, the severity of injury rose dramatically when there were three or more attackers.

Reports such as these are immensely helpful for planning training, with the news reporting on only the most violent crimes such as knife and gun crime it is easy to get side tracked with your training.

Like I have said in the past, train for the violence that is occurring in your area or for the confrontations you are likely to face in your employment.

One of the ways people get distracted with training is through sports events like UFC and MMA. Everyone thought that you needed to learn Brazilian Jui Jitsu to be able to defend yourself as for the past years Brazilian Jui Jitsu was the master of the Octagon. This dilemma even went as far as the United States Military where a large portion of the MACMAP and Army Hand to Hand Combat courses are made up of Brazilian Jui Jitsu ground work. This is now being remedied as troops who come back from Iraq and Afghanistan are saying they need more stand up grappling.

So don't get side tracked in your own training, Train for what you are going to face

Third Party Defence

We all train to defend ourselves, but how many of you train to defend or protect other members of your family. From parents protecting children, each other or as working as a team where one parent is protecting and one parent is escaping with the child or children, to the nanny or Au Pair protecting their employers children.

Third party defence is harder than it seems, not only do you need to be armed with the physical skills what you also need are set drills.

Of course before we get to the latter stages our awareness and common sense must come into play.

Here are a few examples of everyday activities. I want you to answer the questions as honestly either as A) never, B) sometimes, C) always.

1. You are getting into your car or your putting your child into the protective seat. Do you look around you while you are doing this?

    A) never
    B) sometimes
    C) always

2. While you are out with your children in the park, how often do you let them get more than 5 metres away from you?

    A) never
    B) sometimes
    C) always

3. While in a busy shopping area, how often do you let your children get more than 1 metre away from you?

   A) never
   B) sometimes
   C) always

4. How often when your child was/as in a pram did you move more than 3 metres away from them?

   A) never
   B) sometimes
   C) always

5. You take your child to school or your partner to work and pick them up later. How often do let them walk from the car/transport etc into school/work and back again without you escorting them or watching them arrive safely?

   On quiet days   A) never   B) sometimes   C) always
   On busy days   A) never   B) sometimes   C) always

Do you know who is around you?

I am sure you can come up with more situations in your everyday life where your children or partner might be at risk.

For those of you who constantly train in the hard and soft skills I can hear you saying to yourself "but there are too many variables to answer A,B,C" and in one sense you may be correct, but only insofar that I have just put these thoughts into your head.

How many of you actually do what you say on a subconscious level and act on it every single time you leave your home. By this I mean you do not need to be prompted (as above) to be switched on. If you do great, if you don't maybe you will now.

Now let us look at some basic awareness skills.

Do you check: outside, before you leave the building you are in (if possible)?
The immediate vicinity of your car?
The inside of your car before you get in? The entrance way to your house on arrival?
Train platforms/bus stops before getting on/off?

Could you the do any of the above and more while carrying children, bags, pushing prams, when you are tired, when it's dark, raining, arguing with your partner etc.

Remember this is basic stuff. Now what about physical skills

Could you keep an attacker at bay long enough for your family to escape?

Could you keep calm enough to give your partner or older child instructions while defending them from a crazed attacker, would they even listen to you?

Could you get someone out of your car or stop them from getting into your car to hurt your family?

Have you ever done any physical scenario training with family members? Have you practiced defending your child or partner while having to use a pram?

What should your partner be doing while you are defending them? Are the children old enough to run, when should they run and where?

What should you, your partner and your children do if one of them or you are grabbed?

What tactics should you use on buses, underground, in busy environments, in narrow alleyways?

How quickly could someone disappear with your child or partner on a busy street like this?

The list, like individual self-protection is endless and only your experiences and knowledge of violent attacks and how they happen can help you in your training to combat them.

The chances of anything happening to you or your family are very slim, but you can cut those slim chances down even further.

Low Light Training

We are going to look at some aspects of low light training. This normally comes under combat pistol / rifle / shotgun training, but as a lot street violence and home break—ins happen during the dark hours, low light training should form part of any self-protection system.

Even in the most built up areas there are large numbers of dark and secluded places where attacks can be launched from. So we must realize one basic main rule, if it's dark it is dangerous.

Within the low light training package we have to look at internal and external environments and also low light and no light fighting.

Obviously there are more obstacles during the silent hours to hinder us than during the daytime and to make matters worse because of the time of day they seem to be bigger problems than they actually are.

The obstacles we encounter cover both physical and sensory obstacles.

Here are just a few:

Physical obstacles at ground level, low and mid level, head and high level.

No light Low light
Blinding light Shadows
Noise displacement
Distance distortion

Where you live will also have its own environmental idiosyncrasies. For instance where I live it is only one of a few truly dark places left in the UK. No neighbours for a few hundred metres, no street lights for 1½ miles to the west, no street lights for 12 miles to the west and south and the north covers an area of 14,000sq miles with no street lights. When it is dark it is pitch black, when there is a full moon there is good light but again with all the low light problems. With very little population break—ins still happen and the police come past once in a blue moon.

9.20pm lots of shadow caused by trees, bushes and street lights. On the far left corner of the crossroads is a bench with a man sitting on it, it is probably 50m away, you could be on top of him before you know it.

Having good low light training in the UK should be high on the training list as the nights start to close in in October and winter can last until March. At the height of winter it gets dark at 3pm and your left with only a few hours of daylight.

Stats show that street violence rises from 6.30pm and hits a high between 1.30am and 3.00am

Unfortunately we are to a large degree unable to control our outside environment. The only parts we can control is where we actually walk and by being aware of what is happening around us.

Meditations of a Modern Warrior

9.30pm still quit a few people walking home and on push bikes, a lot harder to see people even with the street light, which again is about 50m away. Notice how little light the street light gives off, and people still walk through here on their own, men and women.

This location is Hyde Park in central London, not the safest place to walk after dark

We can control the immediate surroundings of our homes, and workplaces to a certain degree be they gardens, ally ways, parking areas etc. We can also control our internal environments, again home, workplaces, parking facilities etc.

We plan how we want our homes to look and we can choose where and how to park our cars. To an extent we can plan how our workplace looks and if we cannot then we should be as familiar with this environment as we are with our house as we probably spend more time at work than we do at home.

One of the question I ask when conducting low light training is "can you find your around you home, garden, workplace in the dark?

What is the first thing people do upon hearing a noise either in the house or outside? While they are in bed, they put the light on. Before I go on there is a whole different discussion regarding confronting people who break into your home and we won't go into that here.

You should, in familiar surroundings be able to move around without bumping into furniture, making a noise and tripping over things, and you should know where any potential weapons are without groping around in the dark for them in a state of panic. Putting the light on puts both the owner and criminal on an equal footing, unless the criminal has been in your house prior to the attack you should have the upper hand and be able to effectively fight (if you have to) and have the upper hand in a place you should know like the back of your hand.

Part of your low light training should be conducted at home and if possible at other familiar locations. You should get out at night and train outdoors in real environments.

For those that live in rural environments, night vision can play a small role before an encounter takes place. For those of you not familiar with night vision here is a quick description of what it is.

It takes approximately 30-45 minutes for the eyes to adjust to the dark. On the reverse it takes the eyes 5 minutes to become fully adjusted to daylight and other forms of ambient light such as street lights. Colour perception also changes with the onset of darkness.

If you look straight at an object using the centre of the eye or cone region, the object you are looking at will be invisible. This is because the cone region of the eye is not night sensitive. Looking off centre using the peripheral rod cells of the eye which are night sensitive will bring the object which was invisible into view.

Night vision will only help us prior to an encounter, in spotting potential threats. With colour perception altered and the many shades of darkness and greys that abound in the countryside at night, spotting potential danger is very difficult.

One factor that does help us during low light is that speed and any quick movement stands out more than during the daylight hours. Of course this will only help if our awareness gives us the time to react to this movement without startling us.

Like everything concerning self-protection there is a huge amount of information and training techniques that this short newsletter contains, but as long as it gets you thinking then it has done its job.

If you have any questions or require further info then drop me an e-mail, or ask your instructor for advice if you haven't trained in any aspects that I have brought up, or discuss and practice it with your training partners if you train in a group.

Warriorship

We all know how important the minds role is in self-protection. Well before any physical skills have to be used as a last option the mind is the preferred weapon of choice.

Awareness training has been done to death, and rightly so. Brilliant books by Geoff Thompson and other notable martial authors constantly remind us of our first priority, not to get into a situation in the first place. Even I rattle on to the informed and uninformed about it.

This is all well and good but there is a deeper aspect of what we do that is not looked into in any great depth. Since I started training back in 1978 I have built up a rather large martial library and in all this time I have only ever come across one book that covers the subject in this article. The books main title is "Living the Martial Way" with the sub heading "A manual for how a modern warrior should live" written by USAF Major Forrest E. Morgan. This is an in-depth book and a must read for anyone connected with Self Protection.

I am just going to touch on one aspect of the book in this newsletter. You as a Warrior and Warriorship.

This might sound like a philosophical discussion or study bit I can assure you it is not. It has just as much, if not more meaning towards Self Protection than the rest of the none physical skills we train in.

Most people who study fighting systems have at some time been asked "what is the best martial art"? We all know there is no one best martial art. Major Morgan goes on to say that there are only good martial artists and bad martial artists and goes even further to say there are only warriors and none warriors. How right he is.

Above all else we must acknowledge that we are warriors. Look at what we train in, awareness training, physical skills such as punching and kicking, braking bones, dislocating joints and limb manipulation, choking and strangulation, knife fighting, stick fighting, firearms training and ultimately if the need ever arose the ability to end life. Why train to do all of the above if it is not to be a warrior. Regardless of your profession you must think and train as a warrior would.

I hate the terms martial arts and martial artist. It sounds too much like hobbyist. Something you do for recreation, to keep fit once or twice a week. If you are looking to survive your next encounter, you had better believe playing at it won't help you.

It is not only the soldier today who has a frontline. We all have our front lines in a world more violent than at any other time in its history. Police are on the frontline of crime, anyone involved in a profession where conflict plays a role or has the potential to, has their front line and the average member of the public has their frontline on streets where violence is becoming more common and people are becoming more and more desensitized to it.

So how often do you train? Not just in fighting skills but in the rest of the skills that go into training a warrior, training in the Warrior Arts. Look at how the military trains the warriors, most if not all of their training methods can cross over into the field of training a warrior in Self-Protection. Running, strength training, swimming, climbing and assault courses, who knows who you may have to run from and over what terrain you will have to escape over in the future? The urban jungle poses lots of physical problems that you must be fit enough to overcome.

As a bodyguard for the last 17 1/2 years and prior to that an infantry soldier I take my warrior training very seriously. When my work and home life allows I train for a minimum of 1 hour per day and a maximum of two hours. If I am not physically training I am reading about it and if I am not reading about it I am writing about it. This goes on seven day a week. I know some great warrior instructors who will be reading this newsletter who have the exact same mind-set. They do not play at what they do.

Cultivating the warrior mind-set like anything else takes practice. Start today by thinking of yourself as a warrior. Look at your friends and neighbours who are none warriors, what makes you different from them?

Take this analogy. You start off as a civilian, you join the military, you leave the military, you never go back to becoming a civilian you become ex-military. You have tested yourself, done things no civilian will ever do, you become part of a warrior cast that other warriors instantly recognize.

Now look at how you can and should think of yourself as a warrior. Look at the things you put yourself through, if you have ever done a Geoff Thompson Animal Day or an equivalent you will know what I mean. All the pressure testing, sparring, punishing training regimes, injuries to go through and recover from, none warriors would baulk at some of the things you put yourself through. You have tested yourself, done things none warriors will never do, you have made yourself different.

A warrior lives for the now, 24/7 seven days a week, a warrior never knows when his last day will be so lives every day as his last. Adopt this attitude and live a more meaningful life.

I know lots of people working in an environment where conflict/combat is possible or happens on a regular basis or from time to time. Some of these people do not consider themselves warriors or even have the faintest clue as to its meaning.

Warriorship is not an ego trip. It is not walking around thinking you are better than anyone else. It is a deeply personalized attitude, a preparation for combat that shows you the worst and ugliest aspects of life but ultimately lets you live a life of gratitude, respect and courage and perhaps one day to help someone, a none warrior survive something they never could on their own.

Behind the Times

The BBC this week released an interesting article about bystanders having "a go" with the heading "Fight or Flight, would you have a go" and the sub heading "How would you react if you saw someone being attacked in the street".

I find articles such as these interesting for a number of reasons and I tend to look at them from three different angles.

    As an instructor
    As a student
    As an untrained individual

When studying violent incidents on youtube for example, all you can study is the action that is taking place. Sometimes this may be the whole incident, sometimes it is just snippets of a fight, mugging, beating and the like. And that is all you are going to get in a real life encounter when you see or come across a violent incident. You do not know the whole story.

In the above mentioned article, after studying thousands of violent incidents the researcher has come to the conclusion that Britain is not a "walk on by" nation.

I have to both agree and disagree with these findings.

If you study violent CCTV footage what you will notice is that the people who are intervening in these incidents are not bystanders in the correct sense. They are not someone who just happened to be walking by, they are people who are friends of one of the parties who are involved in the incident. Whether they are stopping their friend from getting a beating, giving someone a beating or saving them from police involvement we will never know but one thing is for sure, they are not innocent bystanders.

The researcher does mention this in his report and says that group kinship has a large part to play, but this is misleading to the general public as the intervener is part of the group involved in the incident. This is not clear cut evidence that Britain is a "walk on by" nation. Who would not go to their friends aide if they were having trouble? and go to their aide a lot faster than if it was someone they did not know.

The article also said that people being too afraid to intervene because they are scared was discounted by psychologists. This i have to totally disagree with. Violence scares the shit out me which is why I constantly put myself outside of my comfort zone and strive to become as good at it as I can. Now if it scares the shit out of me and if you are honest with yourself it probably scares you to, someone who trains to deal with violence then how do you think it is going to affect someone who is not accustomed to it.

Would you intervene? Could you intervene?

One point the researcher has failed to grasp lies in the title "Fight or Flight" The title should have been "Flight, Freeze or Flight" and this is the main reason people are reluctant to help and is the same reason people who are in code white succumb to being attacked, they freeze.

Unfortunately most of those bystanders who do act, the "have a go heroes" that we read about in the papers end up losing their lives. They try to do the right thing but are totally unprepared and untrained for what they were getting themselves into.

This is a true story. A family friend saw a man hitting a woman, he tried to intervene and both the man and the woman ended up beating him up. It turned out they were having a domestic, although it was funny being told the story it did highlight the problem of whether to help or not.

As I say on my website, the public are becoming increasingly unwilling and in most cases because of the levels of violence being used are unable to help those in need.

Whilst writing this newsletter I asked a number of work colleagues if they would help someone who was being beaten up. The initial answer was a "yes" or a "maybe" followed by a pause then the same statement, "it would depend on the situation" and this is from highly trained ex-military war vets who are now close protection operatives.

I am not going to say that you should give or not give help. If your trained for violence and the situation is such that helping will not endanger you then of course you should.

You, your training and the situation will dictate whether you will help or not, if you just dive right in because that is the right thing to do then we could be reading about another "have a go hero" in the paper. If you do decide to intervene in any sort of incident then be prepared for whatever may come your way.

Physiology

As always the aim of this article is to get you to ask questions of yourself, your training and your knowledge base.

How often as part of your training do you study physiology?

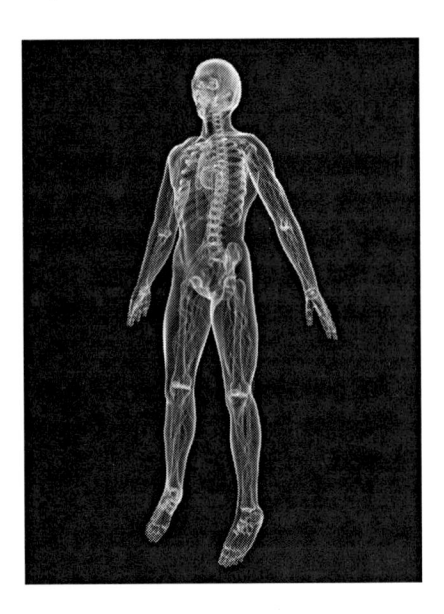

As warriors who study combat a sound knowledge of the bodies systems should be part of your training package. For the study of combat it is sufficient to study those systems that will be affected by what we do to them and how they in tern affect us while in combat.

The systems we need to study are:

    The Skeletal System
    The Muscular System
    The Circulatory System

The nervous System
The Respiration System
Organs Of The Body

Having knowledge of the above systems helps us in many ways, from learning new techniques to actual combat.

Some examples:

From shadow boxing to bag work, pad work to sparring any form of practice that involves strikes, throws and grappling etc, needs to be done with two things in mind.

1. VISUALISATION. For shadow boxing, bag work, pad work, you need to visualise what you are hitting.

Do you just throw techniques and combinations because that is what you have been taught, or do you actually visualise the impact points and the damage caused?

Are you just throwing out shots or are you aiming for specific points, Temple, Eyes, Arteries, windpipe, nose etc.

2. When sparring do you know which muscles are being used and what leverage is required when throwing someone bigger, smaller or heavier? And how is your body balanced so you do not end up on the floor after you have completed the technique.

Do you know what damage your knee strikes cause to the kidneys and what nerve is hit and where it is located that causes a dead leg?

When applying arm and leg locks or joint manipulations do you know what is happening to the joints, tendons, ligaments and muscles, firstly to help you complete the technique and secondly how they all work to stop these techniques when someone is trying to use them on you?

When learning new techniques does your instructor, or do you as an instructor explain the body mechanics behind that technique, thereby getting the maximum speed, power and correct form.

What about your breathing, do you know why you breath out when you complete a technique or when being struck or thrown? Do you know what is happening to the body at that precise moment?

How many major and minor nerves around the body can you name and locate that will provide a quick knockout, escape or make someone comply?

When in different locations, either on holiday or operations do you know how far and fast you can run, how your body functions and what your combat capabilities are at different altitudes and in different climates.

Do you know what damage a stab will cause in different parts of the body and what damage cut will cause in different parts of the body and how deep do these need to be, to be life threatening.

For a fist fight we can learn physically by sparring where to get punched and kicked, how to take them, where to take them and we can harden ourselves against their effects, this can be done at as close to full on as you like.

For a knife fight we can learn where to get cut and stabbed that will cause the least damage to us and keep us in the fight. We can learn about what is happening to the body when we suffer a serious wound. It will give us knowledge of how much time we have got to get help, help ourselves or someone else and can also help us from going into shock.

Although we cannot practice getting cut and stabbed we can practice knife defence techniques with training knives that simulate being cut and stabbed by marking the body with dye.

For a fire fight we can learn how to control the breathing to get shots on target. What fine motor skills are required and how to train them for magazine changes, transition from primary to secondary weapon, quick draws and weak hand drills for when wounded. All nice and easy on the range but add force on force scenarios and the added pressure makes all the difference.

Here are two very easy questions that you should know the answer to: Why do you go pale when you have a shock (fright)?

Why do we get tunnel vision?

These two questions are really basic but knowing how our body works will make you a better warrior, just another part of the jigsaw, keeping you ahead of the game.

Speed

What you do, how you do it and how fast you do it are three leading factors for not getting into a "situation" in the first instance and for that matter getting yourself out of one.

Over this and the next newsletter we are going to look at the "how fast you do it" part. I take it you will have heard of the phrases "action and reaction" and "for every action there is a reaction"; you will also hear some instructors spout the phrase "action will always beat reaction".

Have you ever thought about these phrases or do you just take it at face value that what your instructor says is correct because he is wearing a black belt and is supposed to be an expert. Like I have said in the past, do not be afraid to ask me questions if you have doubts about what I say, question everything.

Look at it this way:

An aggressor is standing in front of you, you react to his actions, but his actions are him reacting to some other stimulus, drugs, alcohol, goading by friends, bad day etc.

Our pre-emptive strike is an action by itself, but it is also a reaction to the stimulus we are receiving from the person in front of us.

The phrase "action will always beat reaction" is not strictly true. The car that crashes in front of you (action) should have every other car behind it crashing as well, pile ups do happen (freeze) but some cars do swerve to avoid the pile up (reaction).

Boxers who throw a jab (action) should connect with that punch every time, but bobbing, weaving, parrying (reaction) makes the punch miss.

There is no definite conclusion to the action-reaction topic, in the end it is the same as the chicken and the egg question, it makes for interesting philosophical discussion but will very rarely help you one bit in a fight.

Though I have said in the above, my argument to the action-reaction theory is that in conflict there are no reactions there are only responses, an answer to the question. My answer to the question is to act before the question has been asked.

I brought this up in a round-about way to look at "how fast you do it" whatever the "it" is, avoiding the situation, punching, kicking, shouting for help or running.

Some people call this "reaction time" I like to call it "action time". I don't want to be reacting I want to be acting, to be ahead of the game. I want to be acting on information that I am receiving ASAP.

The system I teach is the V. I. P. A System, Violent Immediate Positive Action System, not the Violent Immediate Positive Reaction System

So how fast can you "do it"? And how can you train to make your actions faster?

Every piece of information that our brain receives through sight, sound, smell, touch and intuition, that gut feeling that tells you something isn't right (I missed out taste on purpose), passes through filters that stop sensory overload. Some of the information we retain and the rest is stored in the sub-conscious.

Sometimes we will consciously refuse to believe what we are seeing or feeling or what is happening around us because it does not look like what we have trained for, it doesn't feel like what we have trained for though your gut is screaming at you to act, so it gets stored away in your sub-conscious and then BANG game over.

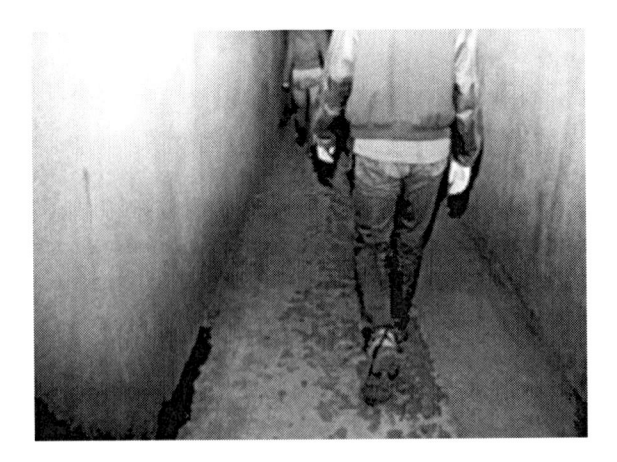

Acting on prior information received at this point in time means your way behind the game. The earlier sensory information you received will have been stored in your sub- conscious for one of the above reasons, if you are lucky it won't be GAME OVER.

I am sure you all have training methods to keep your skills sharp, both physically and mentally. When its time to act we have to GO on the B of the BANG of the starters pistol metaphorically speaking, any longer than that and again it could be game over.

Speed 2

Before we look at some drills for sharpening your responses I want to carry on where we left off last month.

I am a big fan of progressive systems which give us new ways of looking at old problems. Not only do they bring new context to light but they also get us to question what we as instructors and students have been taught and continue to be taught.

One of the newish concepts that has come on the scene in the last few years is the "flinch". Since this concept appeared a number of styles have taken it on, renamed it, repositioned certain appendages of the (technique) for want of a better word and has sort of become a buzz word in the self- protection arena.

Carrying on with "how fast you do it" from last month this is why I do not teach the flinch.

- * It is a natural reaction (remember there are no reactions in combat) only responses.
- * It is defensive in nature.
- * It is taught as a presumption to being surprised.

Now I know there are a lot of unaware civilians out there but damn, there must be a lot of unaware cops and military personnel out there as well, because when I have attended seminars where this has been taught or have watched it being taught it is always at close (closer than handshake) range. Way too close to be standing near someone in a confrontational environment, cop, military or civilian. Even if due to your work you need to get hands on an individual, you need not be closer than handshake range until you decide to close the gap.

So here is some food for thought.

I want you to consider your body as a ship with your conscious mind as the Captain. The conscious mind only takes up to 20% of the power of the mind, but the conscious mind is the Captain of the ship on the bridge, the decision maker.

I am not going to name or explain all of the different parts of the brain and all functions they oversee, they are important when dealing with this issue but for this newsletter I want to keep things simple.

The rest of the mind is made up of other officers of the ship.

Chief Engineer = heart rate, respiration etc.

Radar = movement, co-ordination, reflex actions etc.

There are lots of other officers of the ship with specific jobs that keep the ship running smoothly without interference from the Captain. These parts of the brain are called the sub-conscious or non-conscious mind.

The Captain (conscious mind) knows how the other parts of the ship work on a basic level but cannot run each specific station.

The Captain (you) cannot choose to stop your digestive system you cannot choose how many cells are destroyed and made each day. You do not control your body temperature and this is where the ship fails with the flinch. The Captain is not making the decision!

The argument for the flinch is that as a natural reaction to a perceived threat it cuts out the decision making process so the reactions are faster.

Non conscious impulses travel up to 100,000mph depending on the length of neural pathways. Impulses in the conscious brain travel at around 120mph.

Meditations of a Modern Warrior

Look at it this way, Radar pick up an unspecified incoming threat, they inform the engine room. The Chief Engineer decides to put the ship into full reverse without telling the Captain (flinch), which is what happens in the above paragraph.

The problem with this is that the radar and the engine room cannot see the specific threat. The Captain, when informed can look in the direction of the perceived threat and can make a corresponding correct answer.

100,000mph in the wrong direction or 120mph in the right direction. I don't know about you but I don't want my chief engineer making decisions for me.

Look at the types of flinch
- hands raised
- Ducking
- Freezing
- Blinking
- Head turning
- Jumping
- Crouching

You may do one or more of these and they are hard wired into your system. You cannot change the way you flinch and you will flinch the same way for every perceived threat that comes your way.

You can override the flinch through training, thereby making your response times faster.

Realistic conditions, use of opponent's personal cues, anticipation of actions, zoning in and changing your attention focus all help in your decision making becoming faster and positive. This is regardless of simple choice responses, multiple choice responses, stress, fatigue and anxiety when deciding on the decision to be made.

There are lots of different flinch reactions and the one thing everyone has in common when flinching is that you are going to get hit, the problem is you just don't know where that will be. Put a weapon into the mix and you compound the flinch factor even more.

You need that gap, a pause for however short a space of time to make the best judgement you possibly can, and even so we are still talking about milliseconds.

With a conscious decision you still know you will get hit, the difference is that now you decide where you will get hit to minimise the trauma and keep you in the game. And if your Action Time is on the ball you may just escape unscathed.

I had started to write about various drills to enhance your response time but as I was writing it became apparent that trying to explain the drills so you could understand them was more difficult than I first thought and would possibly consist of a chapter of a book or more than likely a book in its own right. So I'm afraid you will have to either train with me or find someone who can take you through this part of your own training.

The Perfection of Technique Through the Totality of Presence

Mushin, no-mind, many people who train in any form of warrior art have heard of it, I like to think of as "The Perfection of technique through the totality of presence".

There have been a few times in the past while either defending myself on the street or competing, when the fight was ended by me using a technique that I did not know I had used. Only once on the street as friend was rushing to help and after watching the competition video footage did I find out which techniques I had used.

The totality of presence can apply to all walks of life but we shall stick to technique for this newsletter.

At any given time during your day do you know where your mind is? For that is where perfection lies.

Does your mind wander when you have no specific task at hand, do you shut down and think of nothing, day dream or think of future events?

Be honest when you answer this question.

Do you let your mind wander when:

    A. You are at work
    B. You are training
    C. You are bored

The totality of presence is you, your mind and your body 100% experiencing the now.

The situation you are in at any given time, good or bad will never come again, you cannot make that time up. That experience and the chance to learn from it should be taken, not shied away from.

How many times in the past while training have you become bored and started to think of other things?

How can you expect to achieve perfection if you aren't even there.

Training is the place where we perfect our technique, make ourselves fitter and stronger. We need to fine tune everything for that single moment when it all must come together. This is the one time when the totality of presence cannot be found wanting.

Bruce lee said "I fear not the man who has practiced 10,000 kicks once, but I fear the man who has practiced one kick 10,000 times".

The totality of presence must be there in every training session no matter where that training session may be, indoors or outdoors. It's wet or windy, your ill or tired, your carrying an injury, your in unfamiliar territory or abroad and cannot speak the language and even though we train for a lot of possibilities there are a million and one things that reality can throw at us that we cannot train for.

Take any technique and start off by do it 1,000 times, everyone at full power and as correctly as possible even if you start to get tired. Focus on every part of the technique, from whatever standing stance you use concentrate on the body mechanics. Feel which muscles need to relax and which need to tense, how different parts of your body need to move, how does your balance shift when you move. Concentrate on the contact point and then the retraction of the weapon and back to the starting position.

When you feel your mind wandering stop the exercise and note down how long it took to get into Mushin, how long you stayed in Mushin and how many reps you did before you were no longer there. Write down everything you noticed while deep in concentration.

Some people will think that muscle memory will come into play. This is not so, we are talking about training the mind to focus on the now.

When protecting yourself the presence of totality will free your mind, you will hit targets that you do not see with your eyes as if the technique has thrown itself, your techniques will flow smoother and your body will be more relaxed. You will think more clearly and be able to make faster decisions.

The Totality of Presence is the art of changing our brain waves from Beta to Alpha and doing this quickly as possible.

Edged Weapons

Here we are coming to the end of the year and despite all of the government and police amnesties, crackdowns and stiffer prison sentences, the knife is still the preferred weapon of choice for attacks on our streets.

So January sees VIPA Tactical Training kicking off the year with an Edged Weapon Defence Workshop.

Let me ask you first, do you train against many different types of knives or do you just have 1 or 2 generic techniques?

Knives can be grouped into three categories:

> Fixed blade—the blade does not move
> Folding blade—the blade folds out from the handle
> Sliding blade—the blade slides out from the handle

These three types of knives can be found in nearly all of the following classifications, they can be either:

> A weapon
> A utensil
> A tool
> A religious implement
> The can be pointed with blunt edges (poignard, stiletto)
> Single edged
> Double edged
> Single edged with half serrated edge
> Serrated
> Hooked
> Short Long

Apart from knives you can classify swords, axes, screwdrivers, broken bottles, knitting needles in fact anything with a point or an edge and made from any material as an edged weapon.

When dealing with knife attacks we have to remember two major points.

> Firstly—expect to get cut
> Secondly—you can survive (more on the « survive » word below) an edged weapon attack even after serious injury.

Most edged weapon defence programs start off in one of two ways, the bad (poor techniques and not much knife awareness) and the good (knife awareness and then good technique).

Obviously the good is better than the bad but they both miss out on two factors that without knowledge of can still get you killed if you are armed with the latest awareness and technical abilities.

These two factors are physiology and psychology.

Physiology with regards to wounds and the effects they have on the body and psychology with regards to the wounds and their effects on the body and the psychology of the attacker.

This next paragraph may seem a little off topic but has a larger part to play in edged weapon defence than in the unarmed arena so please stay with it.

I mentioned above the word « survive »; I used to like this word and used to use it. I also used the phrase « nobody ever wins a street a fight; both parties will have injuries they will have to deal with ».

I stopped using the above so long ago I can't remember when i last said them. They don't belong in my warrior philosophy anymore, they are just wrong.

The word « survive » is negative and gives the same implication as « trying ». Trying is for losers, you have heard the phrase « you should be proud, you tried your best » said to someone failing or coming last etc. Forget trying (surviving) and focus on winning.

Winning your next encounter

Winning against edged weapon

And if you pick up some cuts and bruises along the way the positive mental attitude of wanting to win and winning will be more helpful in any recovery.

OK back on topic.

As ever with these newsletters i want you to look at your own training and to get you to start asking questions.

So letus look at the knife first. As I said above knives come grouped in different categories, look at the pictures below, how would you defend yourself against each one? do you need specific techniques depending on the format of the weapon and the tactical situation you are in at the time or would your 1 or 2 generic techniques cover everything.

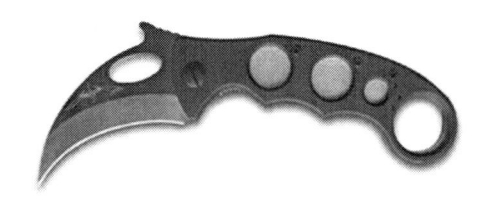

Meditations of a Modern Warrior

Do you practice attacking with various edged weapons?

I am not talking about knife fighting. I don't teach this to UK civilian's, it would be irresponsible of me to do so. What I am talking about is becoming familiar with the body mechanics with regards to various objects.

You will get a better idea of the angles of attack, physiological target areas and how they are hit, how and why you may get hit by an attack and how you may take a hit in an area to keep you in the fight (something else not generally talked about)

Studies show that the slash is the most common strike and is used prior to a stab.

Defensive wounds were found in 15% of those who suffered a single stab wound and around 54% of those who suffered multiple stab wounds (Hunt and Cowling 1991). Point to note, these figures are quite old and so may have changed.

There has also been bruising around the chest and shoulders where people have been forcibly pinned against walls or floors.

As most people are right handed, wounds tend to appear on the left side of the chest as it is a bigger target, is closer to the attacker and contains numerous vital organs.

The biggest killer of a knife attack is shock. If you can overcome the shock factor of getting cut or stabbed then here are some up to date facts.

Given that you are a normal person in good health with a normal heart rate, blood pressure, lung capacity etc. and you can compress the wound, then unconsciousness and death occur when the following areas have been haemorrhaged:

Timings are approximate

Carotid Artery 2-20 minutes
Jugular Vein 15-60 minutes
Sub-clavian Artery 2-20 minutes
Sub-clavian Artery 15-60 minutes
Brachial Artery 5-60 minutes
Femoral Artery 5-60 minutes
Any part of the heart 1-2 minutes
Popliteal Artery 5-60 minutes

Of course these timings will differ with regards to each individual. But you can fight and win against an edged weapon.

Edged Weapons 2

There are a variety of techniques available to successfully defend ourselves when either threatened or attacked with an edged weapon, but the technique does depend on the actual weapon being used.

Because the defensive techniques are weapon specific it brings into play the physiological aspect of the appendage being used in the technique.

As we know we are probably going to get cut or stabbed, the defending appendage is likely to be one of the first if not the first parts of the body to be affected as it attempts to deflect the attacking limb.

We therefore have to be aware of any major (arteries, tendons, ligaments) and minor (cuts and flesh wound) areas that may be affected by trauma and could cause loss of use to that particular body part.

We also need to be aware of the tactical situation as this will also have an affect on our overall choice of what to do.

As wrong as it sounds we need to close with the attacker (see ranges below). This enables to bypass the weapon as we deflect and immobilise it.

Staying at a distance where we are in range of any thrusting or slashing attacks as in a fencing dual (see ranges below), is definitely not the place to be and is obviously where most damage is going to be caused.

The ranges below are also the ranges we will be dealing with, with regards to firearm disarming.

0-5 ft Advantageous to both parties
This is the range where, armed or unarmed everything will take place; it is in this close contact environment that we need to be comfortable with.

We can deflect, immobilise and bypass the weapon at this range. We can also pre-empt any attack.

Attacks and threats of an attack by the attacker can be made instantaneously.

5-10 Ft Advantageous to both parties
This range gives the defender the option to run and gives more time to make informed decisions. Longer range defensive weapons can be used here as in walking sticks, canes and umbrellas. Also throwing weapons should be used from here. The attacker can cover this distance in two quick steps so the distance can be closed to 0-5 ft quickly. Shouting and gesturing with the weapon to cause the defender to freeze is employed at this range, and capitulation is more than likely to happen here. The defender is not in total control of the situation at this range.

10-15 ft Advantageous to the defender
This range gives us the opportunity to run, call for help and put obstacles between ourselves and the attacker.

Of course these ranges are only a starting point. A lot will depend on the attacker and defender. Health, fitness, body shape, combat capability, reason for attack or tactical situation, defending of oneself or others etc. You can work out for yourself your own ideal ranges and what you can do from those ranges that you find preferable.

Example: Downward X block

In the VIPA System there is only one defensive technique that is used that does not do any damage to the attacker. Every other defensive technique is used in an attacking fashion and is called an "Attacking Stop"; it damages the body part it hits, like any other form of attack.

In a blocking sense the X block is just not the right technique to do in this or any other situation. But as an Attacking Stop, against an upward stab, close in 0-1ft with the attacker possibly grabbing a shoulder, it can be used to attack the nerves and muscle along the inner forearm.

As each stab comes in, the arms in an X fashion with the right hand over the left hand, are pumped downward to attack the arm holding the knife. Note: after each attack both arms are retracted out of range of the knife. After two or three attempted stabs the attacker will feel pain in the muscle and nerves of the inner forearm and his attacks will falter, obviously for people with higher pain thresholds it may take a few more attacks to affect the arm. Once the attacks start to falter that is when the arm is immobilised and a counter attack (whatever you are comfortable doing) is implemented straight away.

This is the simplest way to explain the technique without demonstrating it and the picture below does not convey the downward attacking motion, just the mid-point at contact. Try it for yourself and see how many upward stabbing attacks your training partner can do before pain stops the attack.

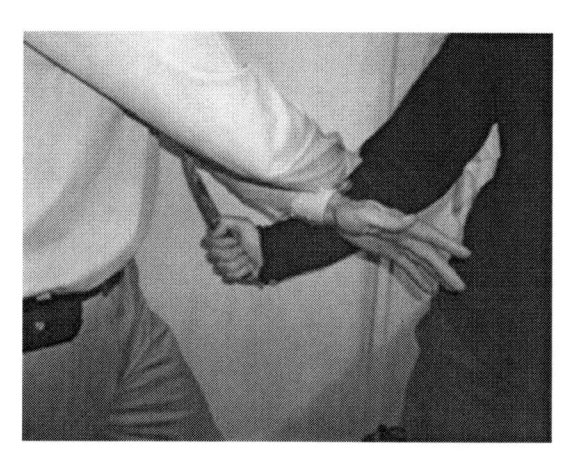

PISTOL DISARMING

The first Close Protection Combat Systems Workshop of 2011 in January deals with close range gun (pistol) attacks against a principal. These techniques are for Close Protection Officers working in an unarmed environment and although the techniques are technically the same as when defending ourselves, certain parts of the techniques have to be altered when defending others.

Different techniques are used for semi-automatic pistols and revolvers. You need to be able to disarm a pistol that is already drawn. You need to be able to disarm a pistol while it is being drawn from a hip, shoulder and thigh holster or from a waistband or pocket.

President Reagan moments before the assassination attempt.

We will carry on next month with pistol disarming for the Close Protection Officer.

Close Range Gun Attacks

Before we get on to the subject of Close Range Gun (pistol) Attacks I want to take a look at the tragic shooting on the 8th of January in the USA targeting Congresswoman Giffords and the random shooting of 18 other people who were close by. Some of whom sadly lost their lives.

All shot at close range, 4ft at most with a Glock 9mm pistol.

The gunman ran towards the congresswoman and her aides from the rear of the queue. One eyewitness claims the gunman must have had some range time as his accuracy and calmness did not suggest someone who was hyped up and shooting wildly. After the Congresswoman was shot he walked down the queue of people waiting to see her and shot members of the public at random. It wasn't until he had to change magazine that three individuals restrained him.

Time Line of Events.

1. The gunman walked to the front of the queue to speak to the Congresswoman. An aide told him to go to the rear of it, over 20ft away. This is just prior to the shooting.
2. The gunman ran from the rear of the queue up to the Congresswoman and shot her from a distance of no more than 4ft.
3. The gunman walks back along the line of people shooting at them until he has to change magazine.
4. As he stops firing three people jump on him and restrain him until the police arrive.

The Signs of the Attack

1. When the gunman walked to the head of the queue he was noticed by an aide. How soon? As approaching or as he got close? He was forgotten about as soon as he walked to the rear of the queue.
2. As the gunman ran the 20ft past everyone in the queue to get to the Congresswoman it was not regarded as suspicious by queue members, even though he has already walked past them once to get to the rear of the que and maybe even twice as he walked to push in at the front. No one responded to the gunman drawing the weapon from either a pocket or from the waist of his trousers and firing the first shot.
3. No one attempts to defend themselves or anyone else as the gunman walks and shoots people along the queue. He walks nearly the 20 feet to where he started off from.
4. Realization that the firing has stopped, people respond.

Although no one is to blame we can see the classic unaware (code white) state of the queue members in their environment. Once the shooting had started everyone went into the "Freeze" state of the Fight—Freeze—Flight model. The typical thought of "This can't be happening" which to the untrained person puts the brain into neutral and does not allow any cognitive thought to take place. Even though the gunman was at close range (see ranges below) No one in this state would be able to respond. Once the gunman stopped firing the "Freeze" spell was broken and people responded.

Close Range Gun Attack (Pistol Disarming)

The first VIPA Close Protection Combat Systems course of 2011 deals with close range gun (pistol) attacks against a principal. This course is aimed at Individual bodyguards and 2 man teams and deals with Close Protection Officers working in an unarmed environment or as you will see in the ranges section below it may be quicker at this close range to use an unarmed response rather than going for your sidearm.

Although the techniques are technically the same as when defending ourselves, certain parts of the strategies, tactics and techniques have to be altered when defending others.

Different techniques need to be used for semi-automatic pistols, revolvers and machine pistols such as the Ingram M10 - M11

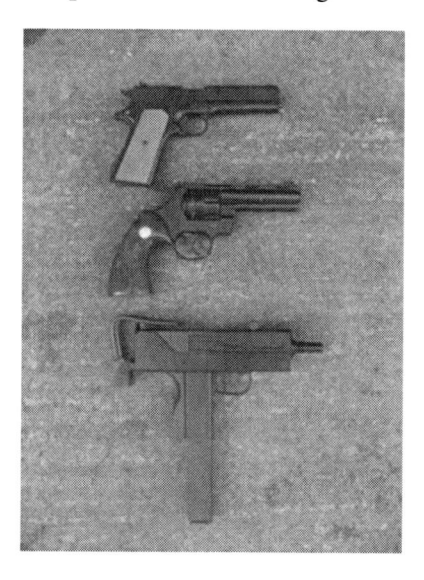

You need to be able to disarm a pistol that has already been drawn, you need to be able to disarm a pistol while it being drawn from various holsters - hip - shoulder - thigh and you need to be able to disarm a pistol that is being drawn from a waistband or pocket

Most people will never have seen a firearm in real life, let alone used one. This can be a major factor as the normal reaction (note: not response) to any close by, loud noise is to duck.

Most people who teach gun disarm techniques fail to pass on this one piece of information on, and it is that as soon as you start your disarming technique the weapon is going to go BANG! The weapon being discharged is what we must expect to happen.

If you start your gun disarm technique that you have been practicing in your training class but you have never been that close to one when it is being fired, then when you duck or looking away there is a greater chance of you losing control of the weapon, antagonizing the gunman more and possibly paying the highest price.

In the above incident people ducked, then laid down or hid behind trees, the natural "flinch" reaction took place.

The BANG! Has a larger part to play in gun disarming techniques than you think. If you are unfamiliar with firearms then go to a range and get used to them. If you live in countries like the UK then go to clay pigeon shoots or places where you can shoot .22 weapons, anywhere where you can become familiar with the BANG!

RANGES

There are three ranges to consider when dealing with firearms. These ranges will give us either 1 option or presents us with a number of options and can be beneficial to both the attacker and defender.

0 - 5ft

In close quarter combat this is the range where everything happens, armed or unarmed. It is where we can take some control of the situation before any technique is performed. It is advantageous to the defender as they are already in a position to neutralize any threat in front of them.

5 - 10ft

This range is advantageous to the attacker. The range is not too great that the aim is going to be affected. The gunman has control of the situation and the defender has two choices.

1. Close to a range of 0 - 5ft and attempt to disarm
2. Move away to a range of 10 - 15ft and escape

10 - 15ft

This range is advantageous to the defender. Unless the gunman has had range time, then hitting a target at a maximum range of 15ft or more while the target is moving is extremely difficult.

President Reagan moments before the assassination attempt, note how many law enforcement are looking inwards. Area where the attack came from.

The main difference in technique with regards to defending others and defending ourselves are:

1. Body alignment
2. Angle of deflection
3. Body cover
4. Closing the distance

Body Alignment

Moving the body out of the line of fire is imperative when there is only ourselves to think about. If the technique goes wrong and a round is discharged, then as we have moved offline the round should miss us and we can attempt another disarming technique.

For the Close Protection Officer this is not an option. Staying online in the line of fire while attempting to disarm the weapon shields the principal from the attack (hence the term bullet catchers), gives the principal time to put distance between himself and the attacker and if other close protection officers are present gives them time to give the principal body cover.

Angle of Deflection

The angle of deflection marks the area of space where you will deflect the weapon into before disarming. The deflected weapon must not invade the same space into which the principal and any other close protection officers are making their escape for obvious reasons, and only practice and training as a team will give you this instinctive application.

Body Cover

We have already mentioned body cover above. This can be achieved in a number of ways.

For the Individual Bodyguard there are a number of options such as placing their body between the attacker and the principal while attempting to disarm the attacker, pushing the principal to one side while attempting a disarm, thereby giving the attacker two targets to choose from thereby slowing down the thought process. For two man teams see Closing the Distance below.

Close the Distance

Unlike protecting ourselves when at ranges of 5ft and beyond when faced with a firearm, where our first choice if possible is to put more distance between ourselves and the gunman, the Close Protection Officer again does not have this option. Depending on the tactical situation on the ground, at some point either an individual bodyguard or the Personal Escort Section of a two man team is going to have to close the distance with the gunman. This again gives the gunman the choice of two targets, keep shooting at the principal and maybe the bodyguard will get close enough to attack the gunman. Or shoot at the closing bodyguard and then hopefully the principal will escape.

As you can see the prospect for survival if working in an unarmed environment is not good for the bodyguard having to deal with the gunman as training and tests have shown, though in most cases especially with more than one bodyguard the principal was able to escape the killing area.

There is obviously more to this subject than this brief outline can cover, but we will come back to it in the future.

Vehicle Security

As part of the Civilian Self Protection Training Program we include a Security Awareness Course. This is as a stand-alone training day and some sections are also included in the 'Be Your Family's Bodyguard' Course.

The Security Awareness Lectures and practical sessions include vehicle safety, from the viewpoint of the family and other people who look after children.

With the amount of distractions that surround us today, driving, approaching the vehicle, Embus—debus (getting in and out), traffic light and stop sign awareness among other things, are all pushed to the back of the mind.

Crime around the vehicle and especially carjacking only happens when the vehicle is static, crimes will include the taking of the vehicle, Kidnapping, robbery and in some instances especially overseas the unfortunate victims have been also been murdered.

While the vehicle is in motion we have the opportunity to spot any potential hazards while approaching junctions and car parks etc.

The most common areas for carjacking are:

    Parking next to the ATM
    Traffic lights
    On busy roads, vehicles parked or stuck in traffic
    Car parks
    Road junctions
    Home driveways

Meditations of a Modern Warrior

Below are listed a number of carjacking incidents from the UK, South Africa and Brazil:

Former Aide to the Queen Mother carjacked—Battersea UK
Kirsty Gallaghers Mother carjacked—Surry UK
Waste removal van carjacked—Rochdale UK
Woman carjacked—Edinburgh UK
2 Separate carjacking incidents—Glasgow UK
Woman carjacked—Lancashire UK
Woman carjacked—Banstead UK
3 Separate carjacking incidents—Sydenham UK
Jenson Button—Sao Paulo Brazil (Brazil has major carjacking problems)
Woman killed in taxi carjacking—South Africa (SA has major carjacking problems)

As you can see from this short list carjackers will target any vehicle. The UK listed incidents above are just from this year

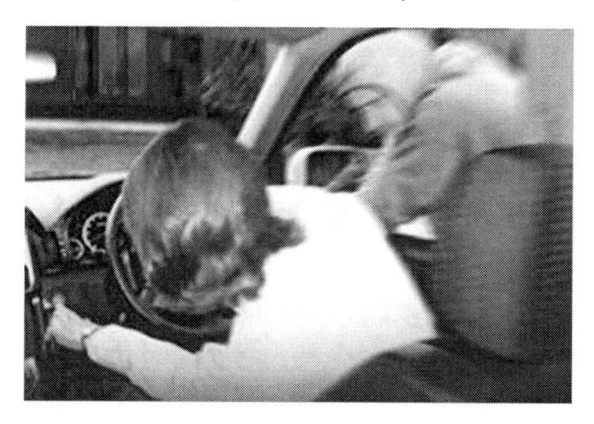

Carjackers will target certain individuals. This will be through an opportunistic attack or by surveillance.

The rich and famous (obviously)
Parents with children
Business vehicles
Vehicles that display wealth with valuables on show.
People who are car jacked while in their vehicle make it easy by:

Driving with the doors unlocked
Driving with the windows down
Driving with loud music playing
Driving with valuables on show
Unaware of surroundings—vehicles following, pedestrians on the pavement
Parking or stopping near groups of people

People who are carjacked while approaching or are around their vehicle make it easy by:

Unlocking vehicle from a distance with the remote
Leaving vehicle doors open while putting items in the boot
Leaving vehicle doors open while putting children in the rear seats
Leaving keys in the ignition while doing any of the above

The former Aide to the Queen Mother (listed above) was kidnapped taken to an ATM where he was forced to take out money. He was then taken home, stripped and beaten. These types of crimes where people are taken with their vehicles for a short period of time are commonly known as a quicknapping

We all drive and do things around the vehicles at some point like the lists above suggest, but there is a time and place and if you are aware these can be done safely.

There is more to this than what is in this short newsletter but I hope it gives you some idea of how and why people and their vehicles become targets.

Pre-Post Fight Mental Battle

How prepared are you to overcome the pre-post fight mental battle?

This is concerned with what is commonly known as the 'aftermath'. Everyone, be they a civilian, in law enforcement or in the military have a set of 'Rules of Engagement', guidelines by which you can operate within the law when having to defend yourself. And herein lies the problem, these 'guidelines' are open to interpretation by people who will judge you, people who probably weren't even there when whatever happened, happened and you had to deal with it.

It doesn't matter how many witnesses there are because each one will tell a different story, each one will have had a different view from a different angle, so will have seen a different picture. Each one will have seen whatever happened from along a different time line, some may have seen all of it, some parts of it and some may only have seen you looking like the aggressor.

In nearly all instances the police will take you and whoever else was involved to the police station and until they have conducted their investigation you will be looked at as a criminal. You may even be charged with an offence. This is not a dig at the police it is just how things are.

If the thought of going to the police station worry's you then what if you are charged with an offence and have to go to court?

Guilty or not your name will appear in the local newspapers, if it is serious maybe the national news. Are you prepared for that degree of intrusion into your life?

How will this affect your employment, your family and family life?

Are you mentally tough enough to inflict serious or lethal harm to defend yourself or your family if there is no other course of action, how much time have you given to playing things like this out in your mind, or talked to family and friends about certain situations you may be fearful about and what are their thoughts on what you should or should not do under certain circumstances?

The macho answer to all of this is of course "yes I am prepared", but unless you have come to terms with the consequences then that is all it is, a macho answer.

If you are in a dangerous occupation, live in a dangerous area this can become something of a nightmare. We have all heard of and understand the effects of Post Traumatic Stress Disorder but here we are getting into the realms of Pre Post Traumatic Stress Disorder which can be just as debilitating, and of course if you are worrying about this while engaged in an incident then it could be lethal for you.

"Why didn't I do that, why didn't I do something"

"what if this happens?, what if that happens?, what if I do this?" puts your brain in neutral and puts you in the 'freeze' point of the flight—freeze—flight model.

The bad guys are not thinking this, they don't care. As decent people we do care but to be able to care we have to come to terms with what we may have to do well before the event.

If we don't then it could be game over.

Where would you prefer to be, at court or at your funeral?

As Geoff Thompson said "Dead or Alive-the choice is yours".

Home Security

Home security has been around for centuries. From the owners of medieval castles who built high walls, large steel gates, moats, ramparts for soldiers, had murder holes in walls to pour scalding oil on any trapped enemy who had gained entry to the castle, escape routes and well lit corridors.

The Japanese used a flooring system called a nightingale floor, whereby the floor nails would rub against a clamp to make a chirruping sound when walked upon. In the quite of the night this was an ideal security alarm system.

Just like todays security systems these castles used multiple layers of security for safety.

A murder hole above a main gate on a medieval castle

Once again this week here in the UK we see an old couple killed in their home during a robbery. While reading this news article it reminded me just how much as citizens of the United Kingdom we are left to our own devices when the time comes to protecting ourselves, our loved ones and our property. Today's lawmakers will try to prosecute us as much as protect us after the fact, if we have had to defend ourselves.

As an executive protection professional part of my job is the planning of trips to overseas destinations. Part of this planning consists of researching and conducting threat assessments on locations that are being visited.

While conducting a threat assessment not so long ago for a trip to the USA, to one of the most, if not the most violent city over there I came across a story of a home owner who killed an intruder with a samurai sword. After the investigation no charges were pressed against the home owner.

In the USA there is a law called the Castle Law (as in and Englishman's home is his castle). This law gives the person the legal right to use deadly force to defend that place and any other innocent person legally inside it from violent attack, or an instance which may lead to a violent attack. This law not only covers the place where you reside but also protects you if you are attacked in your car.

This law has a few back up minor laws included within it, one of which is the 'Stand your ground' law. This law gives the home owner the protection from any lawsuit that may be filed against them on behalf of the assailant for damages/injuries resulting from the use of force.

At the present time 31 out of the 50 States have this law with the rest using parts of the law.

Compare this to the following law that helps protect the people of the UK.

ERR sorry to disappoint you but there isn't one.

We are left with the same law that covers how we may defend ourselves at any time in our daily lives no matter the location. To add insult to injury criminals can and have taken home owners to court and had them prosecuted for injuries received while trying to steal whatever they can get their hands on. It would seem that at the moment in the UK, an Englishman's home is anyone's castle.

So like every other facet of our lives we need to make our home a hard target and as this is where we are going to be spending a large portion of our lives then we need to man our own battlements, unless of course you can employ people to man them for you.

How much do you know about home security? Implementing a home security system need not cost the earth and should reflect the environment you are in. Remember it is your safety that counts, so if you live in an area where burglary is the norm coupled with high levels of violence, then don't complain if your residence has to resemble fort Knox to keep out those who need to be kept out.

A council estate block of flats

Your security needs to start on the outside of the house. How clear are your surroundings, does the vegetation in your garden give lots of cover, shadows that will hide those who are waiting for you to return home. Here we have people like Jill Dando who was murdered on her doorstep, Rachel Stevens was attacked and robbed by three people who followed her home, the robbery happened as she entered her flat. Countless others have been robbed, raped and killed on their doorsteps or taken inside their homes from outside. Make your approach to your front door as clear as possible with outside lighting that can be left on while you are out or with motion sensors that activate when movement is detected.

As you walk round and through your home look at through the eyes of the criminal. Also look and ask yourself questions, what would I do if this was to happen? where would I go if this happened?, how would I get out if that happened?

How would you approach the house undetected?

Where could someone wait unseen for you?

Where and how would they get into the building?

How long after opening a door / window does the alarm go off?

What valuables can be seen from outside of the house?

Is there a secure room where you and your family can stay until it is safe?

Do you have a landline in all rooms or do you have your mobile with at all times around the house?

What is around you that you can defend yourself with?

What procedures do you have for answering the phone, door?

In a previous newsletter I discussed low light fighting. On the physical side of things this is an essential skill if things come down to defending yourself at night at home. How often have you heard a noise and the first thing you do is you put the light on? This not only alerts intruders to the fact that you have heard something but it puts you and them on an equal footing. If they do not know the layout of your home then they are at a great disadvantage while engaged in combat in the dark. Learn how to move around your house in the dark, you spend a great deal of time there, you should be able to move around without bumping into or knocking things over in the dark.

Your study of home security should include alarms, locks, lighting, CCTV, procedures for getting family out of the house, waste disposal to prevent identity theft. Wherever you live there will always be some risk, but risks can be mitigated with a little thought and planning.

A typical English Village

Do you have a neighbourhood watch scheme? Do you know what you neighbours would do if there were intruders in your home? how would they know that there was a problem? And what would you do if it was the other way round?

Have you considered taking your home security procedures on holiday? While you are on holiday wherever you are staying should be considered your home.

How do secure your room? where do you leave your valuables if there is no room safe or suitable hotel safe?

Everything we do is an on-going process no matter where we are and as threats in your area change so should the security procedures for your home security.

Certain aspects of home security can be implemented by yourself though you may need to seek advice from a professional concerning the more technical aspects of keeping yourself and your family safe.

I am generally a supporter of the Police, the police would advise you to let the intruders do what they want and let them leave. That is sound advice to an extent. If you can secure your family in a room or escape then that is a priority. Unfortunately this is not always possible and compliance does not always mean you will be left unharmed. Myleene Klass was reprimanded by the police for brandishing a knife when intruders trespassed onto her property and tried to break into a shed while she was at home with her child, she and her family are still alive and well, I know what my response to the police would have been. In instances like this though I can only advise you to use your own judgment.

Where you live will have an effect on how quickly the police will arrive to help you pick up the pieces, this may be to start an investigation, put you or family members in a bodybag or to arrest you for use of violence while defending what is yours.

The farmer in the UK who shot the teenagers who had robbed him a couple of times prior to that particular incident was sentenced to prison, now he did shoot them as they were running away so he would have been prosecuted in the USA just as much as he was in the UK, but if he had defended himself and his property while the act was being conducted and within the law he may not have had a jail sentence.

Like the farmer I live in a rural area and the police are around 30 minutes away minimum. Personally I may not even report an incident I will just bury the bodies, it would be a lot less hassle. (For all the police who subscribe to this newsletter that was a joke). But you can see how your location will have a direct impact on your continued survival.

Like always I offer more questions than answers, if you have any questions or want advice about this or any other subject then just ask, I am always glad to help.

Combat Focused

Throughout the UK there has been a spate of people being robbed at knife point on the verge of entering their homes, an area where they presumed they would be safe.

Recently a couple were confronted by 2 men who were waiting at the side of the couples house, both attackers had on dark clothing with one wearing ski goggles and a scarf over his face. They were both armed with knives and forced the couple into their home where they robbed them of cash, luckily they were left uninjured.

Personal robberies in London went up recently and in March there were 3000. This figure does not include any other form of violent assault.

YOUR safety is in YOUR hands and YOU can only be safe when YOU make the conscious decision to protect YOURSELF.

The above capitalised words are to emphasise the fact that your continued safety is all down to you and nobody else. If you don't make that decision someone else will and I guarantee it will not be in your favour.

COMBAT FOCUSED 24 hours a day, 7 days a week, 365 days a year.

How combat focused are you?

Sun Tzu wrote:

If you know the enemy and know yourself, you need not fear the result of 100 battles.

If you know yourself but not the enemy, for every victory gained you will also suffer a defeat.

If you know neither yourself nor your enemy you will succumb in every battle

So how much do you know about yourself to make you combat focused and to further harden an already hard target? well I hope you are already a hard target.

There is no point in knowing everything there is to know about how thieves, murderers, rapists, kidnappers work, if you still go about your daily business as one of the sheep (here I am taking it that you know about sheep, wolves and sheepdogs) in the victim state of mind.

Both of the following procedures are opposite sides of the same coin. The enemy will use surveillance to pick you out as a target, you will use counter surveillance to detect their presence. The wolves (the enemy) see you as a sheep, part of the human flock, easy pickings if you are perceived to be weak, alone, nervous, scared etc. You will become the Wolf and learn how to target individuals, how to follow them and learn when to strike, thereby becoming a wolf in sheep's clothing.

Counter Surveillance and Becoming the Wolf.

Counter Surveillance

We are not getting into the realm of James Bond here, and although this is a major factor in Close Protection Operations, it should also be a major factor in your daily life.

The street / area you live in, your place of work, the places you frequent for leisure activities, they all set patterns of routine. Times, routes, method of transport, restaurants, bars, clubs, shops, school pickups with the kids, in fact everything you do every day of your life will set some form of routine.

Sometimes we can change this, at other times we have to work around it and counter surveillance is how you do this.

Do you know what is normal and what would be classed as abnormal in your area?

Do you know who all the vehicles belong to on your street or what vehicles are regularly parked near the drop off point at your kids school?

Do you notice when strange vehicles are on your street?

Do you know your neighbours, their relatives and friends and who frequently visits their house? Not just immediate neighbours but those further down your street.

While travelling on public transport do you know the regulars who travel at the same time as you? Do you notice when someone different uses the bus/train etc?

Do you walk the same route to work or travel at the same times of day?

Would you know if someone was targeting you on a busy street like this?

Are there any potentially dangerous walkways or paths you take every day, if so at what times, how long does it take you cover the ground, what escape routes are open to you?

It's amazing how many people give their kids good advice about being safe then do the most stupid things themselves.

OK you will see that from the few examples above that this is a huge subject, but one your instructor should have on their curriculum.

Becoming the Wolf

This is a rather controversial aspect of training that is not generally used by instructors and their students, but it is a vital part of learning.

So you have started, or are training in Self Protection, you're reading all the relevant literature, you are learning academically about predators and victims, well now it is time to learn about you.

When you have practiced something again and again over a length of time it becomes second nature. At first it might feel strange or you may feel stupid and have to remind yourself what to do and when to do it. Where and How to sit or stand, park your car, drink your tea (I'm not kidding there), but over time it all happens without you ever thinking about it.

Becoming the wolf is partly about learning about you, where you put yourself in the shoes of the predator. This is an exercise where you pick the target, follow the target and decide where an attack would take place. In real terms this surveillance could go on for days before an attack happens (hence counter surveillance) but this short exercise will help you understand more about predators, victims and yourself than just reading about it.

Pick a busy place, a town centre or train station for example, pick a good vantage point and just sit and watch. Remember you are targeting sheep (victims), who would you choose for a robbery, abduction, rape, who looks alert? Who looks in a hurry? Who is struggling with lots of bags or kids? Who has an injury?

Pick your target and follow them, all you are watching for at this stage is to see if they notice you. If they go into a large shop, you into the shop. If they go into a small shop you stay outside and observe. If they get on a bus, you get on the bus. Treat it as a game and note everything about your target that you can. If at any time you think they have noticed you stop and leave, go back to the start and pick another target. If they do not notice you, you could follow them for a number days, what routines do they set.

At the end of each exercise keep notes, why did you choose them? Why did they notice or not notice you? How and where would you have attacked them.

This is how predators think, stalk and attack their prey.

Let me just say that putting yourself in this position may not make you feel comfortable and you may ask is it morally or ethically correct knowing that somewhere out there right now there is a predator doing just what you are doing, targeting someone, but doing it for real? Well this is not the place to discuss those issues but realize that this is a major training aid to keeping you safe.

Another good exercise is for you just to be yourself. Get someone to follow you and record you as you are out and about. Later, at the end of the exercise as you watch the video you will see all the mistakes you have made in your daily life where you have left yourself open as a possible target. Your instructor should be able to get this organised for you, but you should not know when it is going to take place and you should not know who is doing it.

Learning about oneself is equally as important as learning about the enemy.

Once again I leave you with more questions than answers.

Looking For Wolves

Last month we looked at taking on the role of the wolf, the predator. Choosing a victim, conducting surveillance and finally deciding where and how your victim would be attacked.

This month we are going to look at the predator from a victim's point of view. We are going to take on the role of the sheep and look for wolves.

When it comes to fear, danger or some situation where we can sense something is not right it's our gut instinct that gives us our first warning sign, telling us that something is wrong.

How many times have you said to yourself "There's something about him/her I just don't like" or walked through an unlit or seemingly deserted area when your gut is telling you 'this is not right' but you walk on anyway.

This is part of the victim mentality and one we are going to look at now.

Before we do anything else let's look at some of the types of predators that may be out there, some will be specific to your location and some will be general to all locations.

In this short list I have not put them in any order of severity as that is subjective to the person who is or has been targeted.

Drunks
Beggars
Pickpockets
Robbers / muggers
Thieves
Rapists

Meditations of a Modern Warrior

    Kidnappers
    Murderers
    Terrorists

Of course the list is much longer than this, only you will know what threats you are going to face.

Depending on your location and your job you may come into contact with many types of predators or you may come across one or none in your entire life. Regardless of this you are training to either win (more on the 'win' mentality in the future) or to negate totally or for as long as possible a potential encounter.

Let me ask you this question, What do you imagine your predator to look like?

Is it the knife or the clothing that makes you more afraid?

Many people have preconceived ideas of what the bad guys/ girls look like. During my time in the military there was an awareness poster circulating around the bases of an armed terrorist dressed in jeans, a combat jacket and black ski mask. The wording on the poster read "not all terrorists look like this" Someone had written underneath on this particular poster "But it helps".

Now while being very funny it did bring across an important message, which is that predators cross into all walks of life and do not always conform to your idea of what they are supposed to look like.

Like last month pick a busy area, station, street or shopping mall for example and become part of the flock, we are now on the lookout for wolves.

While you are out mingling on this training exercise you have to start pigeon holing everyone around you. To some degree we are profiling people here, demeanour, cloths, location, everything has to fit, if you think something is wrong (gut instinct) it probably is.

As you are observing, look at who is standing close to someone who is unaware, how long did it take that person to notice someone near them? Did they notice at all?

Who is taking notice of that person's shoulder bag that is open?

Is anyone moving closer or observing too closely the man / woman who is struggling with lots of bags or kids, or moving closer or observing any kids that are around?

Pick out someone you don't get a good feeling from and observe, are they really reading the newspaper? Are they moving around looking at different people? Are they taking too much notice of certain people while sitting drinking coffee at the café?

If there are any law enforcement personnel around observe these as well, you may be surprised to find they are not observing as much as you think.

As you observe try to digest the information you are receiving regarding your gut feeling about someone. What is it about them that makes you feel this way or makes you nervous?

We have all got this wrong at some point, but remember we are not looking to make friends here, the person you feel unsure about maybe a perfectly normal, nice, caring individual, but right now they are a

Meditations of a Modern Warrior

stranger that is giving you signs that you are not sure about. In a real life situation this would indicate that it is time to leave.

Don't forget to look up and study any vantage points, remember this is where you were observing from last month, is anyone taking too much interest in a particular person?

If you are uncomfortable doing this on your own then take a friend, two pairs of eyes are better than one.

Consider the following:

As an executive protection professional I accompany my principal when he is out and about, either as part of a team or on my own. As we move around as part of a team we cover our arcs of observation, within these arcs we scan people in the far and middle ground and observe those in the near ground. This means you have only a few seconds to profile those around you. In those few seconds you have to decide the following, are they a threat, a possible threat or no threat.

While on my own with my principal I now have to manage 360 degree awareness, again it only leaves a few seconds to profile those around me.

If there are any warning signs while there is a team, a team member can cover where that possible threat may come from. While on my own I have to cover where that possible threat is coming from while still keeping 360 degree awareness.

Here we have a number of variations. If I was by myself and not at work I would avoid where I thought a threat might come from. As an executive protection professional I have to put myself between my principal and where the possible threat may come from. If a police officer noticed someone suspicious they may have to approach and question them even though they may be a possible threat.

Remember above I asked you a question about what you think predators look like, well this next tale will show you that some sheep dogs (law enforcement ETC) are just as switched off as the sheep.

Paul 'Rock' Higgins CAS, SAC DIP

The police today in London conduct snap vehicle checkpoints, the same as the military do. While walking along a busy main road this happened just in front of me, so I stopped to watch.

The vehicle was pulled over, a rather beaten up car for the respectable west end of London, and the occupant (Middle Eastern), was asked to get out. Now whether the vehicle came across as suspicious from the P check or just from the look of it who knows, but to the officers in the car there was some reason. As I stood there watching i noticed that the police officer who was interviewing did not have his main weapon with him, that was in the car and his side arm was in a thigh holster in a cross draw position on the left thigh (more on that in the future).

As the officer stood interviewing the suspect he stood facing the suspect's vehicle with his thumbs tucked into his bullet proof vest at chest height. The suspect stood next to the officers left leg (the leg with the holster and pistol), at a 45 degree angle, facing the officer and close enough to grab the weapon.

The officer's partner was still in the police vehicle at this time.

We have recreated this scenario for training purposes employing various attack variations, and every time we have had the suspect go for the officer's side arm the officer has lost.

If there was something suspicious to make the police stop the vehicle then their awareness and training let them down when they exited their own vehicle.

Luckily nothing came of this situation. But is just goes to show everyone has to be aware all of the time. One thing to consider here, they did not notice me standing close by observing, there attention was solely on who they were talking to.

Again I hope I have provided more questions for you to ask yourself than answers.

Actuality Training

A little while ago I coined the term 'Actuality Training' with regards to the VIPA Training Curriculum as opposed to 'Reality Based Training'

If you have been following the news lately both international and your local, you will see that the bad guys have had a busy month, from the top of the criminal spectrum we have had a number of terrorist attacks to the lowest end of the spectrum where the street thugs have been involved in robbery and violent crime. Just seems like a normal month worldwide, but maybe not so normal if it has happened in your locale.

This is where Actuality Training differs from Reality Based Training. Reality Based Training means just that, that the training you are receiving is BASED on what is happening in the REAL world. Notice the words BASED and REAL, we all live in the real world but my ACTUALITY is totally different from yours and your ACTUALITY could be totally different from someone else's.

Look at how different these realities are, civilian, police officer and soldier.

Each one of these requires different training, but that does not go far enough as within each of these three realities there are any number of actualities, job description, locations, age, gender, health, disability etc.

Add to this a person who may have multiple actualities whereby the training they require for their job differs from the training they require in their private life. We are now getting to the specifics of training for our everyday life where even Reality Based Training is becoming standardised for the masses.

Your actuality will dictate the types of training you need to focus on. If you are teaching then knowing your students actuality (see list above for examples) will dictate their Actual Training needs within the framework of your Reality Based Training Program, if you are running one.

When you discuss this with your students or the students bring this up with you, we are in effect here conducting a threat assessment on your student's way of life. This gives us the plan that will focus on the actual training needs for that person.

With regards to yourself, how does your own training reflect your personal actuality? Take for instance your motor vehicle, do you drive a large 4 x 4 with a step up into the cab or do you drive a sports car that you need to step down from the kerb or slide yourself into? Add to this your physiology (only one of the factors to consider) and practicing defence from a vehicle in the general sense will not help you with your personal vehicle as each vehicle and the above examples have their own actuality that require different applications that only apply to you.

Once again I hope I have given you some food for thought.

Programming the Mind

As we all know the mind is more powerfull than any computer in existence today. To attain its full potential, our mind like computers must be programmed to run efficiently, and like computers the mind has to be able to run numerous programs simultaneously.

The conscious mind cannot run these simultaneous programs due to the lack of sustainable concentration as it only uses around 20% of the brains power. The task of running these programs is left to the subconscious mind. But first the subconscious has to be taught which programs to run and how to run them, alongside all the other programs it has currently running such as, respiratory, blood flow, heart rate, body temperature and the destroying and manufacture of millions of cells every day.

These new programms the subconscious has re-install are split into two groups, none combat and combat.

NONE COMBAT PROGRAMS

Mode

> Sureveillance (our radar)
> Recconaissance (seeing what we are looking at)
> Intelligence (understanding what we are looking at)
> Command (our response)

COMBAT PROGRAMS

Mode

> Escape and Evasion (leaving the area ASAP)
> Diplomatic (de-escalation)
> Combat

Before the subconscious can effectively run these programs, they have to be re-installed, re-awakened. We already have these programs built in but they have been made redundant in most people by today's modern lifestyle. Re-installing them is painstakingly hard and takes a conscious effort to constantly practice each individual mode, whereby new neural pathways can be built which will eventually let the subconscious take over the responsibility.

The conscious mind will only take control of an individual program once something has been brought to its attention by the subconscious mind.

Our response to a given situation has to be fast, effective and above all the correct one. In todays fast paced lifestyle with its myriad of distractions, filtering out what is relevant from what is chaff is difficult enough during our everyday lives (none conflict) modes but when it comes to combat, correct responses need to be even more accurate to fully comply with our safety, the law and continued physical and mental well being.

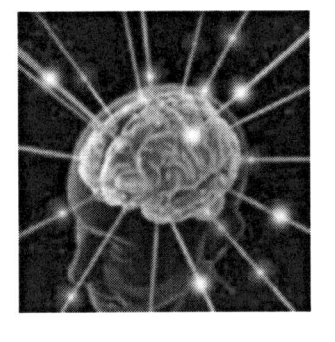

Once these programs have been installed the next question is how fast can you effectively switch from one mode to the other? The none combat modes are easier to switch through, the hardest are obviously the combat modes.

How quickly and how do you train to go from none combat to combat mode? How do get that killer instict where you instantly go cold, become a machine with no feeling for the enemy in front of you?

The combat mode is the only mode that is turned off completely when not in use, every other mode is constantly in use Pre-In-Post combat. These none combat modes let us know when it is time to escape, if your enemy has reinforcements turning up and ultimately when the combat is over. Without these constantly running programs we either do not see other attacks coming, miss the chance to escape or we end up overstepping out position on the force continuum ladder and end up as a criminal.

So let me leave you with this question, how is your computer brain programmed and what upgrades do you need at present to be compatable with your actuality.

Pausing For Effective Combat

How many times have you heard the phrases 'pause for thought' and 'take a step back'? Have you ever been told to do any of them and have you actually ever done them in any situation and if so, have you ever done them in combat and if not why not?

Why is it that in combat situations at close range your strikes and rounds fired miss their intended targets, or after a combat situation when the adrenalin wears off and the pain sets in you find you have been hit places that you would never choose as a target area yourself due to the lack of damage caused in that location?

There is a lot of documentation regarding timing, tempo, and rhythm in combat but within this framework pausing is almost always left out.

The pause is where you make the difference. Look at the untrained fighter raining blows from every angle and without thought. Similarly, the American spray and pray tactic of not aiming but putting lots of rounds down hoping to hit something (no offence to all the Americans, it's just how it was/is).

There is a pause within the whole of our bodily functions and throughout the natural world. Between every ebb and flow there is a pause, at times so small to be undetectable and at times so long it would seem that we are at the end of a cycle and not in an interlude.

We can start as a basic rule with three pauses; a short, intermediate and long pause.

SHORT PAUSE

The short pause may only last for a second or two at most but it is these vital seconds that options are activated or discarded. The pause allows you to actually see the targets you have worked to expose or have become exposed themselves.

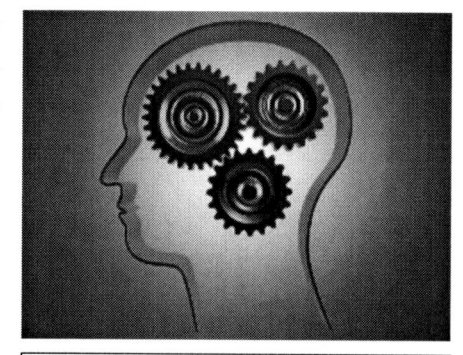

Are your cogs constantly turning?

When drawing your sidearm the pause gives you the chance to see if the target has changed position or if bystanders or hostages have become involved or if you have not muzzled the weapon.

If your primary weapon malfunctions (stops for any reason) the pause allows you to either re-load, transition to your sidearm, or go into a close quarter combat phase.

Strikes with or without a weapon, need to be delivered to inflict injury onto the enemy's most vulnerable areas. The pause allows you to correctly angle the strike use the correct body part and help in planning future moves.

INTERMEDIATE PAUSE

The Intermediate pause in actual combat is where it would seem that nothing is happening for 10-15 seconds. It may be where you are in a grappling situation and you need to take stock of the situation in order to gain the upper hand or to give orders to colleagues or others not directly involved in the combat.

You have a longer time period in an intermediate pause to assess your options; what will I do if he does this? What will he do if I do that? How can I affect this? Is he tiring or capitulating? etc.

This pause gives you the greatest option of seeing when the combat is over, gives you better options of escape or if need be when to escalate the violence.

LONG PAUSE

The long pause can be classed as a lull in battle where you have minutes rather than seconds. You can use this time to steady yourself by employing tactical breathing techniques, to hide, to replenish magazines or to call for help or backup.

The long pause allows you to assess the bigger picture more clearly.

Look for the pause in all your training, from practicing techniques and when they appear in your scenario based training and in any sparring.

Do not confine yourself to manipulating the pause when only in combat, be aware of them in any strategic and tactical training you do and as you go about in your daily life look for pauses in your own actuality. When you make decisions or take any actions, see if you can become aware of the pause and 'take a step back' learn to recognise how you became aware of the pause. See if you can spot where other people should have taken advantage of a pause.

In any environment, in any conditions and at any time, day or night take advantage of the seconds to spare.

Do you know where your target is?

The pause is where you make things happen, where you predict and manipulate future event's. **To the warrior a pause is not an empty space, it is space where you can <u>make</u> time count and it is a vital part of combat.**

Discipline and Motivation

Discipline affects all aspects of your life; working life, personal life, training and how and what choices you make.

One of the biggest problems with discipline, like the rest of your skills is maintaining it. We all have lapses from time to time, when we are down, depressed, tired or stressed and these are the times that disciple is needed more than ever.

Hand in hand with disciple is motivation, the desire you have to do a good job, better yourself, train or study harder, longer, achieve more and become more.

People generally fall into two categories, those who can disciple and motivate themselves and those that need disciple and motivation from friends and colleagues; intrinsic and extrinsic discipline. There are times when even the most self-disciplined and motivated need a little help.

For **WARRIORS** discipline and motivation are essential and never more so than in combat, but let us backtrack to the beginning to see how you can become disciplined and motivated.

Your profession is in some ways secondary to the mental task of you becoming disciplined and motivated but the knock-on effect of these two skills only enhances your profession.

DISCIPLINE PERTAINS TO:

- Self
- Fitness
- Appearance
- Health
- Demeanour
- Work

How you portray yourself to the world tells everyone how you are on the inside. If you do not put any effort into how you look, hold yourself, and communicate with others then when you have to excel at your job or on the field of combat (wherever that is) then you are not going to measure up.

You are going to fit in with one or more of the groups that I have the pleasure to instruct; civilians, law enforcement, military and close protection operators. Look around you, how many people at work and in your training group try to excel all the time. There are those that inspire us, those that do just enough to get by and then there are those who you look at and think "How the hell did you get to do the same job as me?"

It is the first and last group of people that should make you disciplined and motivated. You need to study individuals within these two groups. We all need someone to aspire to, someone who projects the ideal of what we are trying to achieve ourselves. What are their habits, do they rise earlier, work later, how do they go about planning their day or weeks? If you have someone at work or in your training group who falls into this category then talk to them, find out how, why, when, what if etc. about how they do what they do.

Do the same with those who least inspire you, remember you don't want to be like them, these are the typical sheep. Tap into their non-achieving mentality, why is their desk at work always full of clutter? Why are they always late for training? Why do they never push themselves? Keep notes on the differences between the two.

If you work or train on your own or have difficulty finding someone to inspire you then pick out someone who has excelled in their field or in whatever you train. Research will furnish you with information you can use to alter your current mental state. Set yourself tasks and stick to them, do projects or train when you are tired or preoccupied with something else. Learn a new job related skill or train in something you do not want to train in. If you have friends who work in your profession or with similar training philosophies but are not in your local area, then give them a ring, discuss options, strategies and ideas for motivation.

Set each other tasks and make a competition of it. Create accountability among your new contacts you will be doing them a favour as well.

Discipline and motivation like everything else takes practice, it is easy to say "I'll do it tomorrow," Put in that extra hour at work or in the training hall, that extra set of crunches, the last few minutes of a sparring/grappling session even when you're tired, you want to stop and give in, you have had enough. If not: that's where losers and the sheep stop. **If you want people to be inspired by you . . .** Well, you know what to do:

- **LOOK at others around you- who are the leaders, who are the sheep?**
- **STUDY what to do and even more, what NOT to do!**
- **ASK & OFFER to work together.**
- **WORK**

"Great and good are seldom the same man"
—Winston Churchill

"I do not know anyone who has got to the top without hard work. That is the recipe. It will not always get you to the top, but should get you pretty near"
-Margaret Thatcher

Force on Force—Realistic Scenario Training

What percentage of your training is given over to force on force training against learning strategies, tactics and techniques?

We can all stand on the range and convert rounds to empty cases, practice dry drills, kick and punch the bag or pads or train with a partner perfecting techniques. This though is not training for combat.

The last paragraph in the VIPA course brochure reads:

Don't fool yourself into thinking you can handle the threats, the pressure or the pain of an encounter. If you have not trained and gained the skills to win in combat you probably won't. Your life is worth more than that, if you have any doubts about your ability to avoid or win in an encounter then training for the worst case scenario is the only option.

The above statement is so true. If you want to learn how to fight, armed or unarmed, you fight, period. That is not to say that once you have learned the techniques of your combat system you forget about practicing them, all that changes is the percentage of time that is given over to keeping those techniques sharp.

When was the last time you actually trained force on force in some of the following places:

    Your car
    In a lift
    On stairs and in stairwells
    On the bus or tube
    In your home
    In open spaces
    And against various opponents both armed and unarmed.

The list of locations is endless and so are the permutations.

Today it doesn't matter if you are male or female, if you are in the wrong place at the wrong time could get to your feet and escape from this situation. Have you trained for it?

Although your strategies and tactics are primarily dictated by your body type, combat system, environment and job description etc. Force on force training will give you a platform for working out the details that flesh out your strategic and tactical plans.

Force on force training bridges the gap between practicing techniques and real life combat.

Effective force response in relation to whichever force continuum model you are working from is critical in an adrenaline loaded combat situation.

The brain processes around 400 billion bits of information every second but we are consciously only aware of 2000 bits of information per second.

The stronger the neural pathways are in the brain the faster that decisions will be made, but even fast decisions are prone to errors.

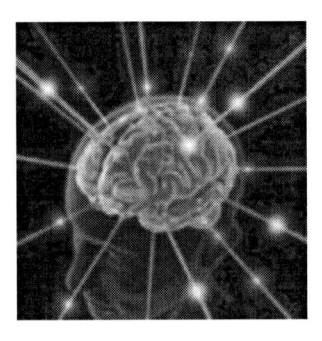

With the above two paragraphs in mind we have to train the brain to recognise what the information being fed to it actually means. The cognitive process is a way of producing the final decision out of several alternate choices from interacting with the surrounding environment. The environment we are talking about here is the environment of combat. If you have never been in this environment you are not going to make the right cognitive decisions (responses), you may not even respond at all (freezing) because your brain cannot evaluate the actions that are unfolding before it.

This is where force on force training comes into play by putting you in the combat environment, effectively giving the brain a set of recognition codes that when needed in actual combat will help speed up your decision making, negating the freeze factor and raising the chances of you winning the combat exponentially.

As civilians, law enforcement and military personnel, how is your training going to help you if a Mumbai type of attack happened where you live. Will you be responding because of the correct training you have received or will you panicking like the rest of the sheep.

Compartmentalization and the Art of Disambiguation (Split Personality)

To win on today's personal battlefield we have a number of aspects and more than one personality to make up what is known as our self.

We are not talking about compartmentalization in the sense of organising our minds to contain problems which need to be sorted out in the future, however long that may be. Compartmentalization in this way enables us to concentrate on problems that need to be dealt with immediately without interference from other sources. What is being described here is one of a number of coping mechanisms which can be applied in either a positive or negative way to help with difficulties we sometimes have to face.

Our self is made up of a number of aspects and each of these has a job to do. In our relatively peaceful lives some of these aspects can and do cross over into other aspects domains. Our personality shapes these separate aspects.

There are a number of models that can be looked at relating to personalities and are generally classed into preference and type, though there are one or two others.

'The big 5' (below) is a simple version of Cattell's 'The 16 basic personality factors'

Personality Indicators:

- Neuroticism
- Extraversion
- Openness

- Agreeableness
- Conscientiousness

These are broken down further but that is not relevant here.

What is relevant is that we need to realise that we have one personality that has been developed through different stages of our growth, learned through touching, sensing, feeling, learning etc.

As we grow we take on different roles that require aspects of our self to fulfil.

These aspects can be grouped as follows but the list will change with regards to who is filling it out.

Example:

Son—husband—father—lawyer—(warrior)
Daughter—wife—mother—midwife—(warrior)
Son—doctor—(warrior)
Daughter—police officer—(warrior)

The personality is not emotional or intellectual it is actual, the aspects are emotional and intellectual and it is these aspects that make the decisions within their domains based on experiences and values gathered through the life that has been lived.

There is one place where none of these aspects have any function and they fail time and time again with so many reported murders, kidnappings, rapes etc. It is within the sphere of combat.

There is no room in combat for the mother, father, son, daughter, doctor, there is only room for the warrior, a separate personality with no aspects to this self, just the cold uncompromising focus and understanding of what needs to be done, with no thought of remorse, no thought of dying or of missing loved ones, that is where the none warriors aspects cause indecision and then they end up dead.

This goes beyond Orson Well's 'doublethink' where you can hold two contradictory beliefs at the same time and accept both of them.

You may believe in the sanctity of life and are prepared to take a life if the need arises but that is the thinking behind living in the peaceful society we live in today.

The warrior, kept in his box does not come out in peaceful times, he comes out in times of battle, where the only sanctity of life is his own and where what needs to be done will be done and when the time comes he voluntary goes back in his box until called for again.

This is the most difficult part, training the warrior self, not the public self. Knowing how to bring out the true warrior, not the pretend warrior, learning how to control your personality disorder so it becomes an effective battle hardened personality ready to die for you. Remorse, grief, forgiveness, guilt are not in the warriors vocabulary or mental makeup.

It is the warrior self that may have to do things that the public self could not do, the warrior self can do what has to be done and can live with it, the public self cannot hope to live with these acts of violence towards his fellow man, some aspect of the public self will always be at odds with what has been done.

So what's it to be?

Whether it's this war

Or this war

HOW YOU LIVE IS UP TO YOU.

YOU MAY LIVE PHYSICALLY BUT WILL YOU LIVE MENTALLY?

Kidnapping and Hostage Taking

Kidnapping, either for political or monetary gain, human trafficking or to commit crimes such as murder and rape is thankfully quite rare here in the UK. However in certain locations around the world kidnapping is on the increase, is big business and is not confined to remote areas, with reported kidnappings now being over 30,000 per year with one particular set of kidnappers (street gangs) making an estimated $500 million alone in the USA.

With more and more emphasis put on the more violent crimes and terrorist attacks, such as suicide bombings and shooting, kidnapping has slipped under the radar to become one of the fastest growing crime trends of the modern age.

There are a certain number of different types of kidnappings and only the most newsworthy will be reported, these are typically political, terrorist and the kidnapping of high net worth individuals, these though are not the only victims.

Here is a short list of different types of kidnappings in no particular order of seriousness.

    Political
    Terrorist
    Sex Trafficking
    Parental Kidnapping
    Express Kidnapping
    Tiger Kidnapping

Sex crime kidnapping
Child Kidnapping
Basic Kidnapping
High Net Worth Kidnapping

So who are actually doing these types of kidnappings?

Professional kidnappers fall into two groups, criminals who kidnap for ransom and terrorists who kidnap for religious and ideological aims or political gain.

Opportunistic kidnappers can be those who are mentally impaired, sex offenders or criminal gangs.

Parental Kidnapping by estranged mothers or fathers.

Within all of the kidnapping variables some have similarities and some have distinctly individual characteristics.

For instance the kidnapping of high net worth individuals relies on the fact that a ransom of some amount is going to be paid for the release of the hostage. On the ransom being paid the hostage is released alive.

Professionals who partake in the so called tiger kidnappings will kidnap a family member to force another family member to either commit or help in committing a crime. The IRA used this method when kidnapping a family member to force another family member to drive a car bomb to a location.

Political kidnapping by terrorists may lead to a number of different outcomes. The release of terrorist prisoners in exchange for the hostages, or the public killing of the hostage to make a political statement.

The sex offender and serial killer will kidnap to torture or rape and finally kill their hostage.

Depending on who you are and the location you are living or working in will dictate to a certain extent which type of kidnapper will target you. So the question you need to ask yourself is what are you worth and what is your value if you are the target of a kidnapping, remember this is not only financial value. Looking at the above list of potential kidnapper's, some will need you alive and in the end some will not.

Knowing who you are, your value, what type of kidnapper may target you and how the kidnappers Modus Operandi can differ within each group will give you information with regards to affecting an early escape or to win through hostage survival.

There is a difference between kidnapping, hostage taking and hostages. Kidnapping is the actual event of the taking of the person, either by force or coercion. Once the act of kidnapping has passed the person kidnapped now becomes a hostage.

Hostage taking is where one or more individuals are held prisoner by either criminals or terrorists in a location from where there may be no way of escape due to law enforcement intervention or by terrorists taking hostages to make a public statement and to bring awareness to the public regarding their cause. Banks, homes, schools, prisons and airlines for example have all been scenes of hostage taking incidents.

We are not going to go into this in any more depth here, suffice to say that like all other forms of violent attack your chances of this happening are minimised further by realising that kidnapping does happen and having a game plan in place to counter possible and actual threats. Once again we are talking about knowing your enemy and making yourself a hard target.

Improvised Explosive Devices

When discussing subjects like I.E.Ds people tend to think that these are issues for military personnel. While in the main this is true in respect that the military are facing this threat everyday while serving in combat zones around the world others like law enforcement and other emergency service personnel, executive protection and PSD personnel are likely to face this threat at some point in their career. With terrorism being what it is today the I.E.D is a large threat to any civilian population and is one of the main forms of attacking a either large masses of people, buildings, company's or specific individuals.

In the west we live in a relatively peaceful environment, by this I mean we do not live in or next to a war zone and relatively speaking none of our neighbouring countries are hostile towards us.

I mentioned the above as it bring into context the next point. I was reading a statement by an Israeli gentlemen who on visiting London saw what he thought was a suspect package on the pavement. On reporting it to the police he was asked if he was sure he wanted to report it as it was likely just rubbish and it would take two hours for the bomb disposal team to get there.

Coming from where he did he was obviously astounded by the lax attitude towards what he thought was a threat. The position of their country in relation to their neighbours and their continued existence has bread into them a mind-set that doesn't see rubbish but sees threats, a mind-set that saves lives.

We on the other hand may experience an atrocity where an IED is used to target the civilian population once every few years. Enough time for us to forget the last one and go back to being complacent.

Meditations of a Modern Warrior

So we all need to be aware of these devices to one degree or another, some more than most.

We are briefly going to look at the following headings:

What is an IED
Types of IEDs
How are they made
How they can be delivered
Who is at risk
Detecting an IED

What is an IED

As the name implies an improvised explosive device is a homemade bomb that is made and used differently to conventional military ordinance. They can be made from almost any material found in the public domain and can also be in the form of military grade explosive ordinance and civilian commercial explosives, commonly though these are often combined.

IEDs are used to destroy buildings, kill or injure those in the immediate vicinity, to cause panic, be used as a distraction and to be used as a secondary threat after a main device has initiated (explodes).

IEDs come in all shapes and sizes, from the size of a cigarette packet to a large lorry. The size and destructive capacity will depend on the intended target or victim.

Types of IEDs

There are literally hundreds of different types of IED and depending on who you are, military, law enforcement, executive, celebrity, government body etc, will go some ways to dictate the type and size of IED to be used and how it will be delivered.

To list a few we have:

Roadside bombs
Vehicle borne bombs
Person borne bombs
Pipe bombs
Postal bombs
Incendiary bombs
Explosively formed penetrators
Rockets and mortars
Daisy chain

Pipe bomb with shrapnel

How they are made

An IED needs 5 components to make it work.

These are:

Switch—trigger
Fuse—detonator
Charge—explosive material
Power source—battery
container

Added to this ball bearings, scrap metal, nails, glass or anything else that will cause shrapnel injury's and you have your IED. In the worst case scenario of a poor man's weapon of mass destruction IEDs can contain toxic, chemical and radioactive material to form a dirty bomb.

The trigger is very important for us to be aware of. We may not be able to see what type of explosive and other material make up the I.E.D but what we have to be aware of is how they are initiated, this knowledge means we are not going to accidentally initiate the explosion. There are a number of ways of initiating and I.E.D such as:

By command wire—an electrical firing cable that leads from the device to user (terrorist) activated trigger. The terrorist needs a good line of sight to activate the device at the precise time and be able to disguise the cable so it is not discovered for this to be effective.

Radio signal—The receiver in the device is connected to a firing circuit, press the send on the transmitter and the receiver will activate initiating the device. Here we have mobile phones (as in the photo), wireless door bells and pagers etc. These work on specific frequencies and in the main will not activate from other transmitters, receivers can though be fixed to work on any radio signal within a certain distance and electric blasting caps can also be set off by radio, radar and microwave signals so the use of any mobile communications equipment should not be used in close proximity to a suspected device.

Victim Activated—These devices are designed to initiate on contact with the intended target. Operated by means of movement, pressure release, applied pressure including crushing and trip wire some of which may be added as an anti-tamper mechanism.

Some other trigger systems include infra-red, light, suicide and timed, and within these there are also breakdowns of varying triggering systems.

How they can be delivered

Delivery systems for IEDs are as varied as are the IEDs themselves and as we have seen above the type of I.E.D goes someway to explain the delivery system.

Vehicle

vehicles can be packed with explosive to detonate in some of the ways described above or can be used to fire rockets and mortars from vehicles such as flat bed lorry's.

Mail

Letter and parcel bombs both explosive and incendiary can be sent through the postal services as legitimate post, though this is hard to do with screening procedures involved with mail shipments today. Hand delivered packages are more of a concern and should only be accepted with caution (see below).

Roadside bombs

Roadside bombs can fall into two categories, those that are buried in the road or at the side of the road and those left in vehicles not only cars, vans and lorry's but also on motorcycles and pushbikes as well as being disguised as or within rubbish or implanted in dead animals.

Here we can see the phone, C4 explosive and the nails acting as shrapnel

Placed

Placed IEDs are your typical suspect package (see photo), something that looks out of ordinary or where it should not be. A suitcase, holdall, box, bag etc, milk urns and crates have also been used in the past with the only limitation being the terrorist's imagination.

Would you ring the authorities or just walk on by?

Person

IEDs are used within explosive vests in back packs and on vary rare occasions internally by suicide bombers. Proxy bombs whereby individuals are forced to transport a bomb by vehicle or by themselves with backpacks and holdalls to a specific location by way of kidnapping a family member or blackmail. These can either be an unknown suicide (suicide by proxy) or a non—suicide event.

There are also other ways of delivery such as waterborne but the above are the most common.

WHO IS AT RISK

The risk to individuals from an IED is based a number of factors. Without going into too much depth we will condense the threat down into military and none-military, government and none-government, and criminal. Within each of these groups we have only two groups of targets, mass and specific targets.

Mass Targets

As the name suggest, mass targets are counted as multiple person targets. These can be as small as a 4 or 8 man infantry unit hit by a roadside bomb to a large number of civilians killed by a suicide bomber in a night club.

Car bombs that cause mass casualties are at the moment actively used in the Middle East.

A mass target in a civilian population can involve those who have no reason to believe they are possible targets, this is usually where terrorists are using the event to gain wide media coverage for the attack and their cause. Shopping malls and sports stadiums and recreation areas such as restaurants and night clubs etc, are prime targets.

Military bases where rear echelon services (none combatants) can be targeted to affect troop morale where both male and female service personnel are working and to interrupt logistical operations, daily combat operations and to try to impose restrictions on personnel movements.

Mass targets and multiple casualties in the civilian arena will have a large impact on emergency services, medical facilities and transportation services.

Targeting Government facilities such as places of work and critical infrastructure locations such as power and water facilities can have a number of effects, not only will the bomb cause collateral damage and the loss of life but can have a profound effect on the command and control system that will be in place to specifically deal with this situation.

Specific Targets

When terrorists target specific individuals it is again aimed at media exposure but in these cases it is also to keep the loss of life to a minimum to those who the terrorists see as having nothing to do with their war and who want to gain the support of the public. These targets are classed as soft targets, those that have little or no security, establish routines or believe there is no threat against them.

Specific targets include:

    Politicians
    Judges
    Solicitors
    Diplomats
    Military personnel
    scientists
    businessmen
    Writers
    Newspaper editors
    Criminals

There have also been numerous members of the public who have been targeted with the use of IEDs by unexpectedly falling foul of seemingly trivial arguments which have lead to death threats and onto to attacks.

Detecting an IED

The more complex the IED the more difficult it is to detect. So like everything else in our self-protection toolbox our awareness is what is going to help prevent us from not recognising the threat.

For the military, the advancement in signal jamming whereby a vehicle/s and troops are enclosed in a bubble of electronic frequencies designed to jam incoming signals means that terrorists are using losing low tech command wire roadside bombs more and more.

Use of command wired IEDs means the bombers need to have a few things in their favour, some of which are:

    Line of site to the bomb
    Bomb and command wire must be well disguised
    Route of escape

Some indicators will be freshly dug earth or earth that is a different colour to surroundings, lack of population or vehicle movements, abandoned vehicles that look heavy on their axles for that particular type of vehicle, Dead animals, footballs and other popular western items left on the ground.

Civilians who may be targeted and for protection officers looking after targeted civilians checking of vehicles everyday has to be routine, even in secure parking facilities.

Approaching

> Checking the ground around the vehicle for oil, grease discarded wire cuttings
> Checking the vehicle for scratched around door, bonnet and boot locks and seals, scratches around tyre rims and grease stains
> Checking all doors, bonnet and boot is secured
> Check inside vehicle through windows, is everything where it should be
> All without touching the vehicle

On receiving mail whether it is expected or not:

> Check for unusual or unexpected origin
> Mistakes in the address
> To much postage or labelling
> Smells
> Small holes or tears Grease stains
> Excessively taped package

The information here has not even started to scratch the surface of this subject and I have tried to keep it as basic as possible for those who are not familiar with the subject of improvised explosive devices.

Your awareness to this type of threat whether you are looking at it from a mass (indirect) threat or from specific perspective is what will keep you alive.

'The Now'

> Nothing exists apart from the here and now
> —Bruce Lee.

The 'Now' is where we live, at this exact moment as you read this newsletter nothing else exists, no thoughts of the past, or of the future. Memories of the past, hopes for the future do not have any impact on the space and time that is this exact moment of 'now'.

So why am I mentioning this? Well in the past the newsletters have looked at 'The Totality of Presence' 'A.N.Ts, Automatic Negative Thoughts' and a few interrelated subjects, like most people I read forums, articles and join in discussions with like-minded individuals through all levels of proficiency and experience.

One recurring theme that most new, intermediate and some advanced practitioners of the warrior arts seem to be intent on is the future, I.E post combat and what will happen once the combat has finished.

As far I possible I like to know who my enemy is though this is easier in relation to my work than in my personal life, we need to know as much about our enemy as possible to fully arm ourselves to deal with the threat.

Once we know everything we can about our enemy and then planned and trained to counter the threat then we should not give them any more thought.

There are too many people giving far too much thought about their enemy and what may happen in the combat and post combat phases of the action.

We train our bodies in the here and now to deal with future events but how many of you train your mind in the here and now to deal with the same events? Or do you just worry about what will happen if you do this or that or your enemy does this or that.

We can learn from past events but we cannot predict the future, basing our physical and more importantly our mental combat skills on the many possible future outcomes of a combat situation is a waste of time and energy.

Only one consequence of our actions will (in combat) come to pass, we cannot know what that will be, we can assume a timeline of possible events leading up to that final post combat consequence but what that will be we can never know.

The here and now is what matters, in combat the post events can have a detrimental effect on our combat abilities. We can be led by them, down paths we had no intentions of going, we can be frozen by them and ultimately we can be killed by them.

Too many people are discussing the post conflict phase not as a training tool to be used to their advantage but as a problem that they do not want to face, I keep hearing and reading the same 'but what if' over and over again. Worrying is not problem solving, in fact you do not have a problem until the combat is over, you may not even have a problem then, you may not even be involved in a combat situation for the rest of your life and here you are worrying about any post conflict actions.

Know the possible consequences of your actions, train to deal with them but live in the here and now no matter what the situation.

'On Winning'

Winning and surviving are two completely separate entities.

You cannot win against something you cannot fight; you can survive a car, train or plane crash, you can survive an avalanche, you can survive a hurricane or tornado.

In combat against an enemy; winning is everything.

Both winning and surviving have their place but only one has a place in warfare, and that is winning. Winning is all there is

In warfare it is the winning of the war that is all important to those who are running it. The loss of one or two battles may or may not have an effect on the overall outcome. Battles can be lost but the war can still be won. This is fine in the macrocosm of warfare but that is not our interest. Our interest lies in the microcosm of personal combat; the intimate fight between a warrior and his enemy. An enemy whose job it is to kill him.

This microcosm of war is not just confined to the realms of the professional warrior; it reaches out to everyone in today's violent world.

Our personal wars have a number of battles that need to be won and we need to be victorious in every battle to win the war.

In each of the battle phases, pre-confrontation, confrontation and post-confrontation phase, war is raging on the physical plane but also more importantly mentally, with the enemies of our mind.

If we lose just one of these battles we can end up losing the war. Being physically competent is a given for when the time comes to protect ourselves, loved ones or friends. Then we call forth the skills of the warrior to win in actual combat. The physical is only one battle, not the whole war.

What war?

The war is your life; your way of life and how you choose to live it. What combat tactics are you employing in your life? The mental enemies; worry, regret, fear, hopelessness, outside influences, violence, psychological threats, the list could go on ad infinitum. These enemies are real and the warrior needs real skills and training to win against them. The tactical choice for the warrior living your life as you decide otherwise if you lose one battle you may lose the whole war. The choice is made in your mind.

- SURVIVE
  or
- WIN

If your mind-set is one of survival—then good luck. If surviving (capitulating) is good enough it may mean your body may be functioning but not living. You may suffer depression, anger, live in constant fear, start drinking or become aggressive and violent or dependent on drugs such as anti-depressants. I for one do not want to be spoon fed by my wife for the rest of my life. Do you really want to become a prisoner of war, locked inside a cell of your making via the choices made prior to engagement with the enemy? The terms of imprisonment (some mentioned above) are as varied as there are people suffering (surviving).

Freedom is found by the choices made by the warrior in his personal battles to win the war.

You gain strength, courage, confidence by every experience in which you stop to look fear in the face. You are able to say to yourself, "I lived through that horror. I can take anything that comes along" you must do the thing you think you cannot do. (Eleanor Roosevelt 1884-1962)

Winning the war is everything and the only thing, if it is not, then what the hell are you in it for?

'Bug—Out Bags'

Bug—out bags or crash bags, call them what you will, they all have one thing in common, your survival. They are not Go-bags or shooter—bags or any combination of many types of bag which sometimes tends to happen.

I have seen Bug—out bags of all weird and wonderful concoctions, from bags that are satchel size to a Bergan with enough kit in it takes it takes two to three people to lift it. So when designing your bag, there are a number of factors that need to be considered when choosing what kit and equipment to include. The planning stage has to be systematic in order to get the right tools for the right situation.

Your environment—Where do you live, where are you travelling to, either for work or pleasure? Are you relocating? Each environment has its own idiosyncrasies, its own persona that is sometimes full in your face and at times so subtle that you are in the shit and you don't even know it. Urban, rural, jungle, desert, mountainous, oceanic, hot, cold, humid, temperate, inland or coastal, season changes, population size and demographics, government etc. Everything you can find out about your environment will help determine the threat.

The threat—There are a number of threats that can be condensed into three groups, these are, natural disasters, man-made disasters and war.

Natural disasters—Volcano, hurricane, tornado, flooding, earthquake, brush fires etc.

Man-made disasters—Utility and infrastructure failures such as power, water and nuclear.

War—All out war, terrorism, civil unrest,

These can all broken down further into smaller sub-groups and the more information you can gather the better you can prepare for your immediate survival period.

Immediate survival period—We cannot plan for every contingency and we are not (hopefully) planning for an end of the world scenario so being realistic with time scales is essential. In relation to your current environment or future environment and the threat you may face, what would be the estimated length of immediate survival, 12, 24, 36 48, 72, 96 or more hours?

This is your immediate survival period and what you will carry has to see you through this period, no surprise there. The surprise comes when you get to the end of this period and you are still in a life or potential life threatening situation.

The future cannot be predicted and we have no way of knowing how the threat will evolve, this period has to be used to continue planning the next phase of your survival in the event of the situation going from bad to worse. Break each period down into its own immediate survival period, what will happen in the next 24 hours? What do we do? Where do we go? How do we replenish? And then the next and then the next and so on until you reach your maximum time period. After that, well hopefully the threat has ended or you carry on in the same vein.

Every Item of equipment you have listed so far has been dictated by the environment and the threat. The list you will have made from the above could be quite extensive so now is the time to prioritise everything from the most essential to the least because 'you' are the deciding factor.

You—Who are you? What is your age, gender, height, weight? How is your fitness, strength, health? Are you on medication? Are you invalided? Are you single, with a partner or family, if so how many kids and how old? Do you need 1, 2, or more bags.

The question you need to ask yourself is, how much can I realistically carry, how far can I carry It and for how long?

Once you have the answers to the above questions it's time to pack your bag.

Equipment—It would be wrong of me to dictate to you what you should be carrying in your Bug—out bag, I am not you nor am I in your situation so all I am going to give you here is a list of the essentials that you should carry. What you include and how much you include within these essentials is up to you.

Essentials:

> Water
> Food
> First aid kit
> Shelter
> Clothing
> Fire starting equipment
> Self protection equipment
> Lighting

All equipment you carry after the essentials depends on your personal circumstances.

So you have your Bug—out bag packed, what now? Like any other form of equipment it needs to be tested along with yourself. The best way to do this is to have a scenario from your list of threats, then go out and survive from your Bug—out bag for your immediate survival period, you will find that the way you have packed your bag it is probably wrong, either for comfort and durability, but mainly with regards to items that are going to be used more than others, it goes without saying that your most used items need to be readily available and not stuck at the bottom.

Periodically you will need to air your bag, don't just let it sit there festering, freshen the contents every so often, keep a check on sell by dates, battery power, cleanliness of items, make sure all items work smoothly and are in good condition.

This is as you can see a very basic outline of what is a larger subject but once again I hope I have given you some food for thought.

> I am prepared for the worst but hope for the best
> —**Benjamin Disraeli**

Arcs of Observation for Executive Protection

There are a number of subjects that come under the heading 'Security Awareness', here we are going to look at 'Arcs of Observation' and although we are looking at it from the perspective of executive protection anyone can employ this skill to suit their own circumstances with a little manipulation.

What follows are arcs of observation for the IBG (Individual bodyguard) 2, 3, 4 and 5 man teams.

Before we go any further we need to know what we are looking at and realize that there is a difference between looking, seeing, observing and scanning. One of the main problems is how people 'look', they are either looking and not seeing or hopefully looking and seeing. By this I mean actually taking in and processing the information. I have covered this in the past so I won't say anything further here on that subject.

Our eyes cannot be looking everywhere at once, bad news for the IBG and smaller teams but our arcs combined with a multi-elevation scan helps us with seeing the information.

Breaking the ground into three distances further promotes information processing and here we have the far ground, middle ground and near ground.

We scan the far and middle ground, just like speed reading we use a fast broad sweep of the area. What stands out? Not only possible threats but everyday occurrences, anything that could interrupt the direction of movement or cause any other impediment to your safety. This is all done in the blink of an eye with information processed and either stored, dismissed or acted upon.

Meditations of a Modern Warrior

The near ground needs to be observed. People, vehicles, buildings, the ground your walking on, everything is scrutinised and this also need to be done fast as decision making within the near ground is time critical, so being switched on is essential. As you will see in the diagrams once something is out of your arc of observation it is then another call signs responsibility. That is not to say you dismiss it out of hand as you still need to aware of what is happening elsewhere.

It goes without saying that this is an on-going process with the far ground becoming the middle ground, the middle ground becoming the near ground and so on and so on.

For more than one call sign we now have to get into breaking the area into arcs. Each call sign has their own area of responsibility within the overall 360° observation platform and as each arc interlocks with another call signs arc this negates the possibility of blind spots occurring. Comms between call signs is imperative to maintain a controlled and safe near ground.

If you look at the IBG (Individual Bodyguard) picture you can see how this can be applied in our own personal life, substitute the VIP for your child or partner. Constantly shifting your observation around and making decisions has to be done at a much greater speed and for those new to the industry or for civilians who are new to awareness skills it can be difficult not to look like your head is on a swivel or that you appear to be nervous.

The more personnel we have in the team the less ground each call sign has to observe for any great length of time, this should of course mean that it is easier in spotting any threats or potential threats both direct and indirect but without the correct training on what to look for and how to keep observation discipline, this will prove to be harder and could in fact be detrimental to the operation. Add to this, changes in formation (I have only included some basic formations here) and your arcs will change in relation to formation being used.

You will have noticed that I have not mentioned tactics or any other operational aspects such as personnel movement around the VIP that can impact observation disciple or arcs of fire. As it is a large subject to cover, only the basics have been covered here.

IBG (Individual Bodyguard)

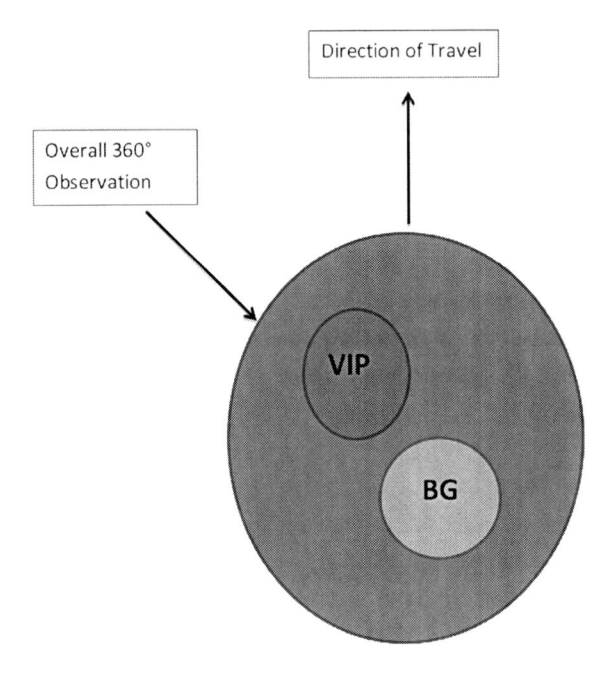

Meditations of a Modern Warrior

2 Man Team

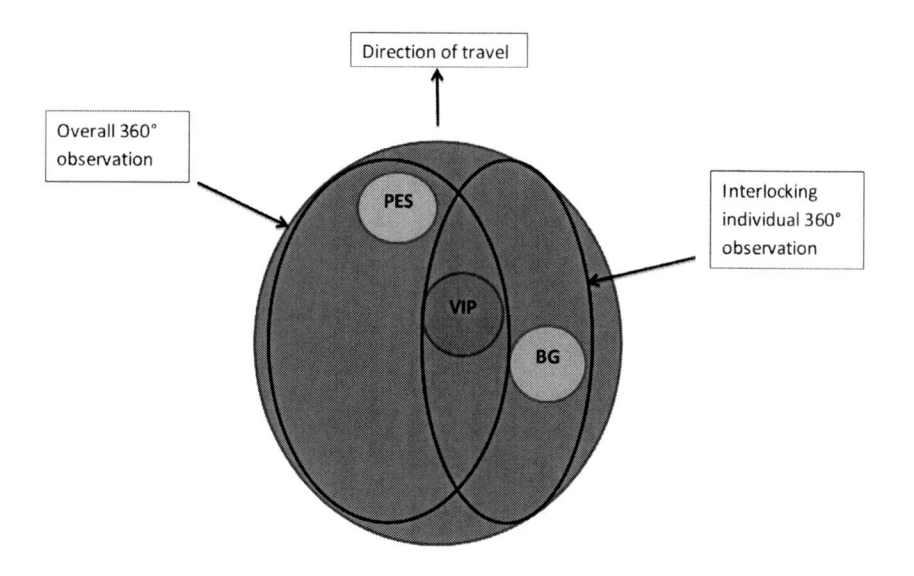

3 Man Team

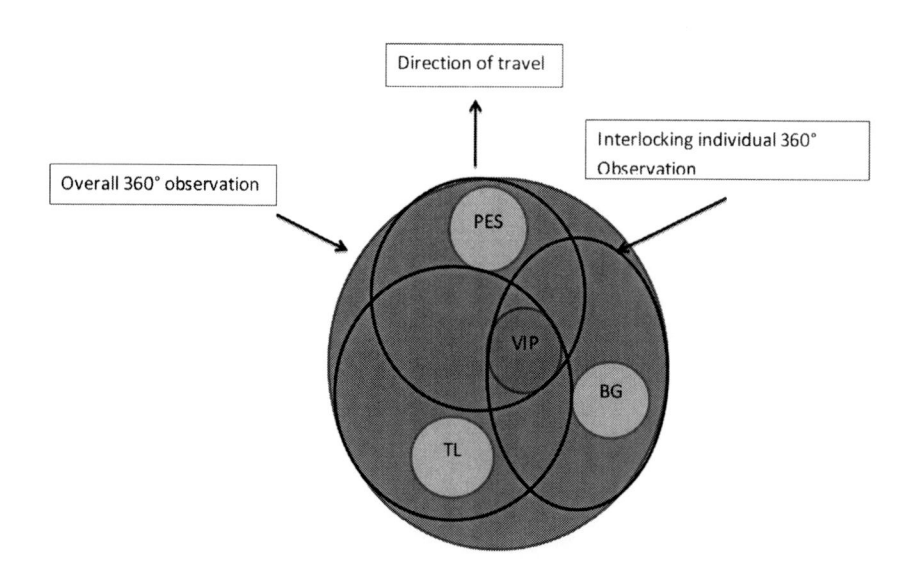

133

Paul 'Rock' Higgins CAS, SAC DIP

4 Man Team

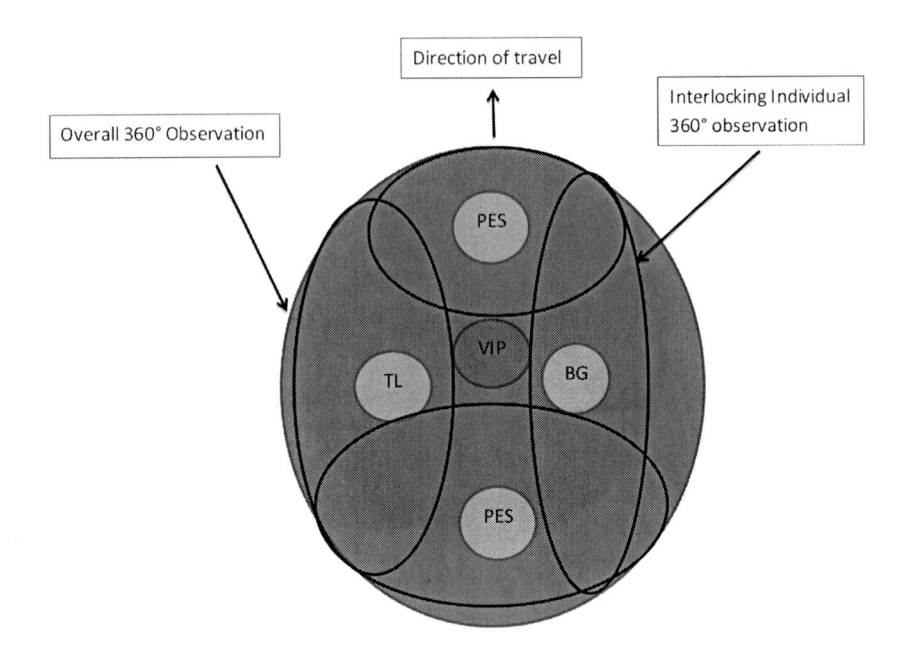

Direction of travel

Interlocking Individual 360° observation

Overall 360° Observation

PES

VIP

TL

BG

PES

Meditations of a Modern Warrior

5 Man Team

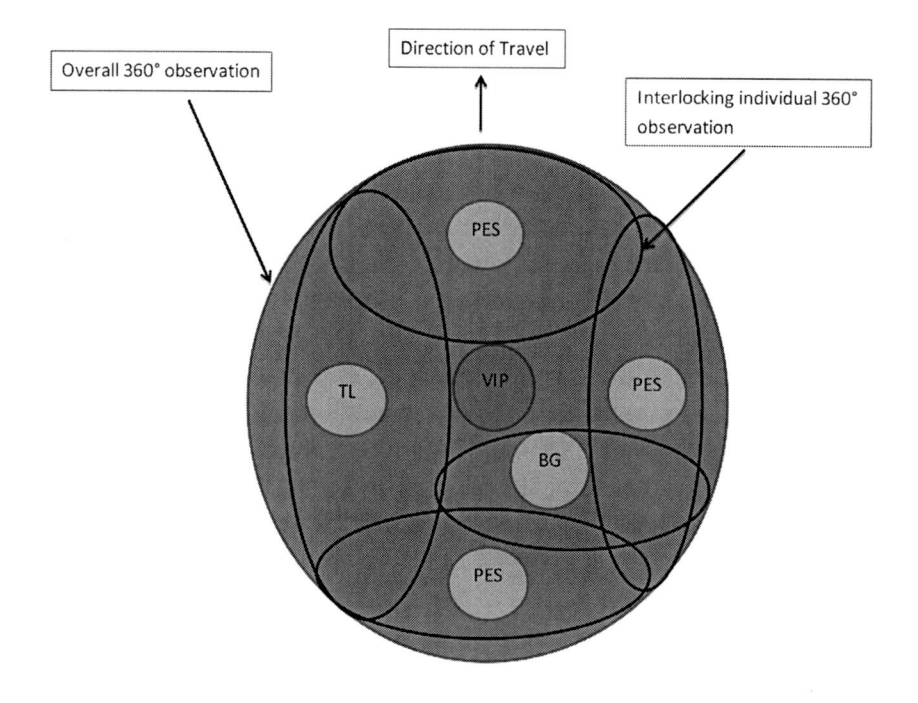

Intelligence is quickness in seeing things as they are
— **George Santayana**

Survival Training

We looked briefly at Go-Bags in a recent newsletter so to follow on from that we are going to briefly look at survival training, something that does not often come to mind when dealing with self-protection and especially for the civilian population.

"Why do I need to do survival training?" is a comment that I have come across on a number of occasions recently, some comments which were made by civilians I can understand but more astounding were the comments by people in the security industry, "What has survival training got to do with Executive Protection?" is a popular one.

I will leave the in-depth answer to that question for a future newsletter. Here I want to pose more questions to get you thinking outside of the box when it comes to self-protection. Just to say that today most of us are world travellers, either for work or enjoyment, who knows where you will be and what will happen on your next trip abroad.

There are many survival courses out there and like choosing and packing our go-bag we need to choose the right one for the location we are going to be living in, working in or visiting but at the start of our survival training we need to look at a generic course that will give us all the basic skills that can be built on later.

Some of the basic requirements include: how to find food, water, shelter, first aid, navigation, mental preparation, direction finding,

The above short list forms part of the base for developing skills that will become specific to you and here it now comes into line with your go-bag or one of your go-bags if you choose to have multiples. Remember you have packed your go-bag for your specific environment.

Each location is going to present you with environmental problems that a generic course just cannot hope to cover, desert, jungle, polar, oceanic, disaster preparedness, hot, cold, dry and wet for example.

I touched on this subject a couple of years ago dealing with short trips in inclement weather when travelling in your vehicle.

Over the last two years the winters in my home area have been steadily getting worse with temperatures getting to -15 at noon down to minus -25 at night. In survival terms this is not too bad while at home or taking short journeys but find yourself stranded with little or no kit, miles from anywhere and things can go from bad to worse very fast.

The training undertaken should be in line with whatever you are doing, working in a war zone (military / PSD) is obviously going to require more training than someone taking themselves off hiking for the weekend. So train accordingly, leaving something to chance is a great invitation for Mr Murphy to turn up.

Build on your base knowledge with new skills for the different locations you are going to be travelling to, get into the habit of asking "What if, What if", it may not be only yourself that needs to survive in a life threatening situation, family members, team mates, employers or people who are travelling in your party may all depend on you for their survival.

Paul 'Rock' Higgins CAS, SAC DIP

Like all the rest of the self-protection skills we practice, getting into the habit of 'doing' is the hardest part alongside realizing what self-protection actually means and what skills come under this very large umbrella.

Ranges

Every weapon we employ in a combat situation be it bodily, edged, blunt trauma or firearm has an effective range which obviously means that to get the full effect from that weapon we need to engage with it at the correct moment within the combat taking place.

Each weapon group has to have its own group of ranges, to explain that phrase let's take the arms and legs for example. A long range kick is employed at a different range than a long range punch and a close range kick is employed at a different range than a close range punch. Easy to follow, you would think but still there is some misconception that we only fight at long, medium and close ranges.

Before we look at the different ranges we first need to know our personal range, this is the space we put between us and someone else so as to be at a safe distance but still within our range capabilities. We should be able to walk up to someone and stop at our exact range whereby we are at the correct distance from the target. Try it with a partner, with a punch bag or against the wall. Every time we stop in fornt or near someone we don't know we should be at OUR PERSONAL RANGE. Your specific body type, your combat orientation (what combat system you use) and how you perceive the people in front of you all have a factor to play in this. It is another skill that needs to be practiced.

If your combat orientation revolves around firearms and edged weapons you should also be quite familiar with identifying ranges for the particular weapon you are carrying.

So let's look at the basic ranges:

- Long Range
- Medium Range
- Close Range
- Upright Grappling
- Prone Grappling

Now we have our basic ranges each weapon system has to be applied individually within these ranges so we have as follows;

Standing Long Range -
firearm
edged
Blunt Trauma
Arms
Legs

Standing Medium Range -
Firearm
Edged
Blunt Trauma
Arms
Legs

Standing Close Range -
Firearm
Edged
Blunt Trauma
Arms
legs
head

Standing Grappling -
Firearms
Edged
Blunt Trauma
All body

Prone Grappling -   Firearms
                    Edged
                    Blunt Trauma
                    All body

You will have noticed that I have only included standing and prone positions, what I have not included here but also does also need to be discussed and trained on as again there are differences within the position / weapon / range matrix is combat when in either a sitting or kneeling positions.

As with knowing our personal range we now need to be able to judge distances for each separate weapons system. So now we know our ranges we need to practice delivering the weapon at the optimal range to gauge its effectiveness, but not only that we also need to practice delivering the weapon at the wrong range, as we all know combat does not often go as planned so knowing what our weapon systems will do at the wrong range, either because we had no other option or because of overriding stress levels the wrong weapon was used at that time, knowing what damage the weapon will cause at the wrong range or what the possible response / reaction may be from an enemy means we can then carry on (hopefully) using the correct weapon from that point on.

Direction of travel and point of impact will also affect the damage caused to a target area when a weapon is used at different ranges and from different positions. Take for example a lead jab or right cross both medium range punches from a standing position. The difference in range and power are significant when thrown from the prone position while on your back.

So whatever weapon system you are training you have to bear in mind position / weapon / range for that specific weapon to be completely effective.

Once again I hope I have given you information that will generate more questions that you need to be asking yourself or your instructors.